THE HAPPIEST
BIRTHDAYS

THE HAPPIEST
BIRTHDAYS

GREAT THEME PARTIES FOR YOUNG CHILDREN

Michaeline Bresnahan
and
Joan Gaestel Macfarlane

THE STEPHEN GREENE PRESS
Lexington, Massachusetts

THE STEPHEN GREENE PRESS, INC.
Published by the Penguin Group
Viking Penguin Inc., 40 West 23rd Street, New York, New York
10010, U.S.A.
Penguin Books Ltd, 27 Wrights Lane, London W8 5TZ, England
Penguin Books Australia Ltd, Ringwood, Victoria, Australia
Penguin Books Canada Ltd, 2801 John Street, Markham, Ontario,
Canada L3R 1B4
Penguin Books (N.Z.) Ltd, 182–190 Wairau Road, Auckland 10,
New Zealand

Penguin Books Ltd, Registered Offices: Harmondsworth, Middlesex,
England

First published in 1988 by The Stephen Greene Press, Inc.
Published simultaneously in Canada
Distributed by Viking Penguin Inc.

10 9 8 7 6 5 4 3 2

Library of Congress Cataloging-in-Publication Data
Bresnahan, Michaeline.
  The happiest birthdays.
  1. Children's parties. 2. Birthdays. I. Macfarlane, Joan Gaestel.
II. Title.
GV1203.B6798 1988   793.2′1   87-34260
ISBN 0-8289-0607-6 (pbk.)

Designed by Trisha Hanlon
Set in ITC Bauhaus and Goudy Old Style by AccuComp
Typographers
Produced by Unicorn Production Services, Inc.

With love to
Tom, Emily, Charles, Mom, and Dad
—M.B.

With love to
Mom, Dad, Bruce, Andy, and Megan
—J.G.M.

CONTENTS

ACKNOWLEDGMENTS

The authors' sincere thanks go to Leigh Sloss-Corra and Miles Bodimeade for their careful and inspired preparation of the cakes and good humor in the face of adversity, and to Christopher and Betsy Little for making the photography sessions more pleasant and productive than we thought possible.

A special thanks go to our models John Aronson; Kay Kawakami; Jason Klauber; Eliza Little; Andrew, Megan, and Bruce Macfarlane; Emily Stanback; James Stuntz; and their parents; and to the model who couldn't make it, Charles Stanback.

We are indebted to Jackie, Liz, Chris, Virginia, Naoko, Candy, Tom, Margaret, our parents, husbands, and children for contributions too various and many to enumerate and thank them for their generous support throughout this project.

HOW TO USE THIS BOOK

Birthday parties are a once-a-year event that is anticipated and remembered. A parent naturally wants to "do it right." Throwing a party for young children is a real challenge, and how to "do it right" is not always so obvious. This book is here to help. It provides specific solutions to the perennial question of what to do with the children. It also has the potential to inspire you to develop original parties of your own. Even the busiest, most inexperienced person can use this book to get the party moving in the right direction and add a creative element that will keep the children enthralled.

The Happiest Birthdays is a collection of "timeless," age-appropriate theme parties. Structured and well planned, they keep the parent in control and the children happy. The introduction to each chapter—entitled "The Plan"—guides you through the "flow" of the party, from beginning to end, including all of the party elements. You can create the entire party yourself with the help of the children, who are actively involved in the creative process from start to finish. Or you can pick and choose the party elements that suit you best. For easy reference, all of these elements are ordered and picture-keyed according to their function—i.e., invitations, hats, activities/games, projects, awards/prizes, and cake/refreshments. Each can stand alone or as part of a unit, and most of them have a life span that extends beyond the day of the celebration—invitations become puppets, magnets, funglasses; hats, decorative projects, and awards become part of a child's everyday imaginary play.

Party Themes

Read through some of the parties and see what appeals to you. When selecting a party theme, bear in mind that although some may seem more oriented to either a girl or a boy, all of the parties have been designed so that every guest has fun! Try to keep your child's guest list to a manageable size. Although very few of us can abide by the age-old formula, "The number of guests should equal the birthday child's age plus 1," it is truly better and easier all around to limit the number. Parties for younger children (2s and 3s) should include parents. For 2 year olds, it's a must; for 3 year olds, it's preferable to have at least a good number of the parents present. Our themes for these age groups involve the parents in the party process. Don't feel that the party has to be long to be good—the opposite is true; 1½ to 2 hours is the maximum party length that we recommend, and nothing is wrong with a shorter celebration that's packed with fun things to do!

Materials

The materials used in this book are for the most part inexpensive and readily available at variety and hardware stores or hobby and craft shops. Since most of the projects require pencil, paper, and scissors, we have not included these in the materials listings. Probably your most important tool is a good pair of scissors. Invest in one, if you have not done so already; it will save you time and aggravation. Tracing paper and cardboard are used to make the patterns and templates for many of the projects, so you should have them on hand, too. The specific amount of materials needed is usually not given, since this depends on the number of guests; we have, however, often given a general guideline to help you in your figuring, e.g., 1 piece of poster board for every 6 hats. We encourage saving scraps and remnants; oftentimes a little piece of something special is just what you need to finish off your creation, and it eliminates one more purchase.

Hats

Unlike the traditional "cone" hat, the hats featured here are very comfortable creations that are rarely just tossed aside! They are designed to fit any head size, simply by untying and loosening or tightening the elastic closure. When you make the hats, try one on your child (or a child of similar size) and adjust the hat to fit; tie the remaining hats to conform to this size, and chances are you'll have to adjust only 1 or 2 hats at most during the party, and that takes about 20 seconds!

Invitations

The invitations all actively involve the child in the party theme. And although all of the invitations can be mailed, some require large envelopes and a layer of cardboard (or bubble-pack envelopes) to ensure safe delivery. You may opt to hand-deliver them with your child—it's more economical and adds to the fun of the whole party experience.

Cake Tips

Eight out of the ten cakes in this book are made from a 9 x 13-inch sheet cake, and we opt for making it from a mix, because of ease and the generally nondiscriminating audience! The final measurement of the cake after being baked is about 8 x 12 inches, due to shrinkage and the smaller bottom surface on this type of cake pan. The cake pattern diagrams reflect this size differential. Always place the pattern on the cake bottom for easier cutting and frosting. Chilling the cake in the freezer before cutting and frosting makes this task easier, too.

Planning Ahead

Taking time to be creative may sometimes seem like an impossible task. But when you think about it, preparing for a party takes time no matter how you do it. If you're not making things, you're still spending time shopping for them! Give yourself plenty of time to get ready for the party. Spreading out the work load helps to eliminate that panicky, "pressure-cooker" state that we sometimes get ourselves into. Most of the creations in this book can be stored flat, either ready to use or with very little last-minute fussing required. You can do much of the tracing, cutting, and assembling work while watching television or listening to some good music. The projects truly are doable!

Enlarging Patterns

We have tried very hard to make everything in this book as simple to understand and accomplish as possible. Wherever we can, we show the artwork full-size, so that you can simply trace it right out of the book. In the cases where you need to enlarge the drawing, you have 2 different options: you can use projection and photomechanical techniques, or you can enlarge using graph paper.

For the first option, there are several pieces of equipment that enable you accurately and quickly to enlarge a pattern; these include opaque projectors and overhead projectors, which are usually available for use through your local library. They will instruct you on their operation.

To enlarge using graph paper, first mark off as many 1-inch grid squares on the graph paper as are shown on the artwork. (The patterns are usually scaled to "1 square equals 1 inch.") Number the horizontal and vertical rows of squares in the margin on the original; then transfer these numbers to the corresponding rows on your graph paper grid.

Begin by finding a square on the graph paper that corresponds to a square on the original. Mark the graph grid with a dot wherever a design line intersects a line on the original. (It helps visually to divide the graph line into fourths to gauge whether the line cuts the grid line halfway or somewhere to the right or left of it.) Working 1 square at a time, mark each grid line where the design intersects it; then connect the dots, following the contours of the original artwork. It's easiest to draw in the straight lines first, if possible, and then concentrate on the curves and angles.

Just remember, birthday parties are happy occasions, so whether you decide to simplify the party themes presented here or elaborate on them in your own way, don't let yourself get so tied up in the details that you miss out on the main point of the celebration—relax and enjoy the fun and festivities along with your young guests! Here's wishing you and your children many happy birthdays and many happy returns!

BEARDAY BIRTHDAY

> **AGE GROUP**
> 2 to 3 years old
>
> **PARTY LENGTH**
> 1 to 1½ hours

Between child and bear, bear and child, there exists a classic chain of love. This is a bring-along party geared to the very young (2 and 3 year olds). Here the basic love linking child and bear becomes a reason to celebrate.

 The Plan

When a child opens the invitation and unfolds Big Bear's arms, Baby Bear tumbles out of a hug. The card informs children and parents of the "bearday" to come and reminds them to bring

a favorite bear to the party. The children will spend many moments selecting a special bear to bring or anticipating the excitement of bringing an often excluded favorite bear pal.

Hanging on to their teddies, children arrive at the party already involved in the birthday celebration. Immediately, have the children and their bears set out on a dramatic hunt for paper Goldilocks dolls. The paper dolls are visibly hidden and easily found. In this way, you gather friends informally for an activity that will extend beyond the arrival of the last guest.

Next, call, "Get your bears!" and seat children, parents, and bears in a circle for singing and applause. The song leader—a parent or baby-sitter briefed fully on the proceedings before the party—can start off the fun with a new version of "Put Your Finger in the Air" (a traditional children's song that can be heard on many recordings), now sung "Put your finger on your bear, on your bear." Have parents help their child put his or her "finger on your bear," "in its hair," "on its cheek," "on its chin," and on, and on. Have the leader encourage parents to sing along, rounding out the chorus of voices. Following the song, the leader should formally recognize each bear for its innate charm, fuzziness, bigness, huggableness, or other bear quality. By ceremoniously awarding bears with a medal and new neck ribbon, you will inspire the children's pride in their bears. Even the most reluctant, shy guest will be undaunted by a round of applause for his or her bear. After handing out the awards, resume the singing with a chorus of "The Bear Went Over the Mountain," as children march their bears up and down in the air, followed by "The Bears Went into the Dining Room." Children, bears, and parents will easily take the hint and follow the leader to the next room for refreshments.

At the table, have parents help the children put on their Bear Hats or Wear-a-Bear headbands. Sing in a punny vein "Happy Bearday To You" and bring out the Bear Cake. Then lead a rendition of the traditional birthday song. Don't be surprised if you hear bear sounds emanating from the full mouths of the children.

Next lead the children to the main party room, where paper Brownie Bear Chains decorate the walls. Cut off individual bears and give one to each child to color with chalk or crayons. With a parent at hand for encouragement, children will work happily and diligently on this project until they are convinced Brownie is perfect. When they are finished, get ready for high jinks. Have three year olds put on Bear Paws and play balloon games (balloon volleyball, etc.). Thrill 2 year olds with lots of bubbles, large and small, blown for them to follow, catch, and pop.

Make free and dramatic play center stage for the rest of the party. Hand out Bear Stick Puppets

and unveil the Two-Story Bear House. The children will know exactly what to do! When they are all "beared-out," give each a Bear Box filled with treats to share with the bring-along teddy, and a collection of favors from the party. They'll leave with a happy feeling that it has been their "bearday," too. After the last child is gone, the birthday girl/boy can settle into some serious unwrapping and enjoy the relatively new experience of the children's birthday party.

The Big Bear Hug

The bearday party invitation comes wrapped in a hug—Big Bear's legs and arms folded to the center around Baby Bear. Don't worry about dropping Baby! Baby Bear is attached by string to Big Bear's tummy. The news is out concerning the bearday and the special guests who will escort children to the party.

Materials: Brown poster board (1 sheet for 16 invitations); white construction paper or drawing paper; black felt-tip pen; string; double-stick tape or glue; envelopes; ribbon for the bow tie (or colored paper or felt).

To make the pattern: Trace the outline of the big and little bears and their stomachs from Figure A; cut out. Transfer the cutout patterns onto cardboard, drawing along the outline; cut out. Use these cardboard pieces as templates for the invitations.

For each invitation: Trace the outline of the big and little bear templates on brown poster board; cut out. Trace the outline of the templates for the tummies on white paper (drawing or construction); cut out. Print the invitation text on the big bear tummy, and the reminder on the little bear tummy. (Optional details for the bear include the paw pads and ear rounds. If you choose to use these, make a pattern and cut them out of the same white paper used for the tummy, or

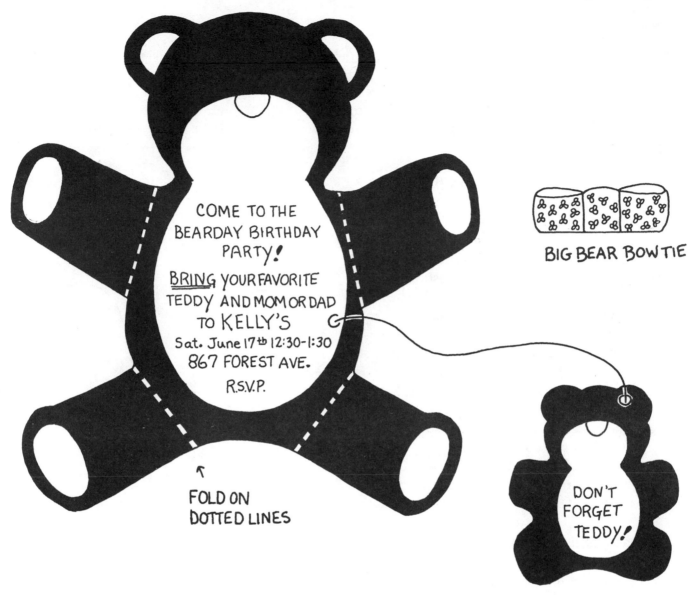

COME TO THE
BEARDAY BIRTHDAY
PARTY!
<u>BRING</u> YOUR FAVORITE
TEDDY AND MOM OR DAD
TO KELLY'S
Sat. June 17ᵗʰ 12:30-1:30
867 FOREST AVE.
R.S.V.P.

FOLD ON
DOTTED LINES

BIG BEAR BOW TIE

DON'T
FORGET
TEDDY!

Figure A

cut by eye, following the drawing in Figure A.) Affix white details to the bears using double-stick tape or glue. Draw nose and eyes directly on the bears with a black felt-tip pen. Make a bow tie for Big Bear out of ribbon (flat or knotted), or draw and cut one from either colored paper or felt. Glue the bow tie in place; let dry. To attach Big Bear to Baby Bear, pass a 2½-inch length of string, knotted in the back, through a needle hole at the side of Big Bear's tummy. Then pass the string through a needle hole below Baby Bear's right ear and knot in the back. Now you are ready to wrap Baby Bear in a hug. Lay Baby Bear on Big Bear's tummy. Crease the arms along fold lines indicated in Figure A and fold them into a hug around Baby Bear.

Text: Come to the Bearday Birthday Party!/ Bring your favorite Teddy Bear and Mom or Dad to (child's name)'s/Date, Time, Place, R.S.V.P. *Reminder*: Don't forget Teddy!

 **Bear Hat**

Here is a simple, effective hat that makes children look like bears! This hat is particularly suitable for the older children in this age group, who can appreciate its costume value.

Materials: Brown poster board (1 sheet for 4 hats); white and black Con-Tact paper; double-stick tape; round-cord elastic.

To make the pattern: Trace the nose, mask, ear rounds, noseband, and earband shown in the pattern section at the back of the book on a large sheet of paper. To complete the band patterns, extend the noseband on both sides of the mask to a finished total length of 16 inches. (The mask should be centered on the band.) Extend the ear-band to a finished length of 13 inches. (The ears should be centered on the band.) A scaled draw-ing of the noseband and earband is shown in Fig-ure B. Cut out the completed patterns. Transfer the cutout patterns onto cardboard, drawing along the outlines; cut out. Use these cardboard pieces as the templates for the bear hats.

For each hat: Copy the templates of the nose-band and earband on brown poster board; cut out. Using the templates, trace and cut a mask and 2 ear rounds out of white Con-Tact paper; trace and cut a nose out of black Con-Tact paper. Put the details on the noseband (nose on mask, mask on band) and earband (ear rounds on ears). Fold ears along the dotted lines at a right angle to the band. Punch holes near the ends of the noseband and tie closed with round-cord elastic. To complete the construction, place the noseband facing toward you (nose front). Hold the earband with ears on the back side of the band, white rounds showing. With double-stick tape, attach the ends of the earband to the noseband at the position indicated in Figure C, forming an arc. The ends of the earband should be flush with the bottom edge of the noseband. (You can sub-

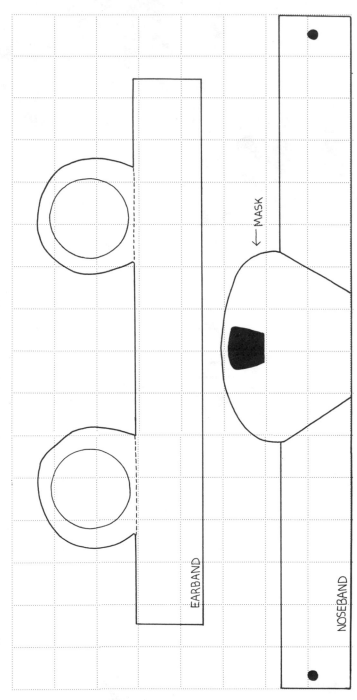

Figure B (1 sq. = 1 in.)

stitute staples for double-stick tape.) A finished, constructed hat is shown in Figure C. Adjust the elastic in the back to fit each child. Hats should be carefully stored—fully constructed—until the party begins.

FRONT
VIEW

SIDE
VIEW

Figure C

cardboard pieces as the templates for the bear headbands.

For each hat: Using the templates, trace and cut out a bear band and a rectangular base band from brown poster board. Trace and cut out of white Con-Tact paper 8 paw pads and 4 ear rounds for the bears. Add these details to the bears. Draw a black nose directly on the bears with a black marker. Glue ribbon or paper bows on the bears' necks; let dry. Center the bear band on the rectangular band. Using double-stick tape, firmly attach the straight section of the bear band to the edge of the rectangular band. DO NOT stick the bears to underlying band; they must stand free. Bend the bears on the fold line. Punch holes near the end of the straight band and tie with round-cord elastic. A finished hat is shown in Figure D. Store flat, untied, until the party day.

 Wear-a-Bear Headband

This headband is the perfect bear to wear, particularly suitable for the very young.

Materials: Brown poster board (1 sheet for 4 or 5 hats); white Con-Tact paper; black felt-tip marker; ribbon or paper bows; round-cord elastic; double-stick tape; ruler.

To make the pattern: Trace the bear band shown in the pattern section at the back of the book on a sheet of paper. Draw or trace upper and lower paw pads and ear round on paper. Cut out. Transfer the cutout patterns onto cardboard, including the interior cut between the arm and leg of each bear (blackened in the pattern); cut out. (Be careful not to cut the bears off the straight section.) Using a ruler, draw a 1½ x 18-inch rectangular band on cardboard; cut out. Use these

Figure D

 **Find Goldilocks**

Whether you take the part of bear or child in this fairy tale, the game will be in the looking. Hide paper dolls, cut from stacks of construction paper (trace a pattern from Figure E), throughout the party room; they should be visible. Bears and children will search the room for them as they act out the 3 bears' search for the intruder. The more paper dolls the better!

Put your finger on its ear, and leave it there a year. . . .
Put your finger on its chin, that's where the food slips in. . . .
Put your finger on its nose, and wait until it grows. . . .
Put your finger on its cheek, and leave it there a week. . . .
Put your finger in its hair, and why not leave it there. . . .

Figure E

Bear Songs

Three classic children's songs have been modified as entertainment for this party. Add a guitarist, if you can.

PUT YOUR FINGER ON YOUR BEAR ("PUT YOUR FINGER IN THE AIR")

Put your finger on your bear, on your bear.
Put your finger on your bear, on your bear.
Put your finger on your bear, and why not leave it there.
Put your finger on your bear, on your bear.

THE BEAR WENT OVER THE MOUNTAIN

The bear went over the mountain, the bear went over the mountain,
The bear went over the mountain, to see what he could see,
To see what he could see, to see what he could see.
The other side of the mountain, the other side of the mountain,
The other side of the mountain was all that he could see.

The bear went over the mountain, the bear went over the mountain,
The bear went over the mountain, to see what she could see. . . .

The bears went into the dining room, the bears went into the dining room,
The bears went into the dining room, to see what they could eat,
To see what they could eat, to see what they could eat.

And they ate all they could eat, and they ate all they could eat,
Of the cake that was on the table, the cake that was on the table,
The cake that was on the table was all that they could eat.

HAPPY BEARDAY TO YOU ("HAPPY BIRTHDAY TO YOU")

Happy bearday to you, happy bearday to you,
Happy bearday dear (child's name),
Happy bearday to you.

 **Bear Paws**

Looking more like bears every minute, children will gladly slip on bear paws in preparation for balloon games. As the children bat away, bear paws give strength to their swipe. This adds a new dimension to games of "balloon volleyball," "keep the balloon in the air," and "balloon catch."

Materials: Brown poster board; white Con-Tact paper; round-cord elastic; balloons.

To make the pattern: Trace the outline of the bear paw, toe pad (all 4 are the same size), and heel pad in Figure F on paper; cut out. Transfer the cutout patterns onto cardboard, drawing along the outline; cut out. Use these cardboard pieces as the templates for making the bear paws.

For each paw: Trace the outline of the paw template on brown poster board; cut out. Using the templates, trace the outline of the toe pad (4 times) and heel pad on white Con-Tact paper; cut out. Stick the toe and heel pads on the paw as shown in Figure F. Punch holes in the paw according to the placement in Figure F. Tie round-cord elastic (roughly 8 inches long) in a loop through the holes, knotting on the back side of the paw. Have a child try the paw on to determine the size of the elastic loop. Make 2 paws for each child.

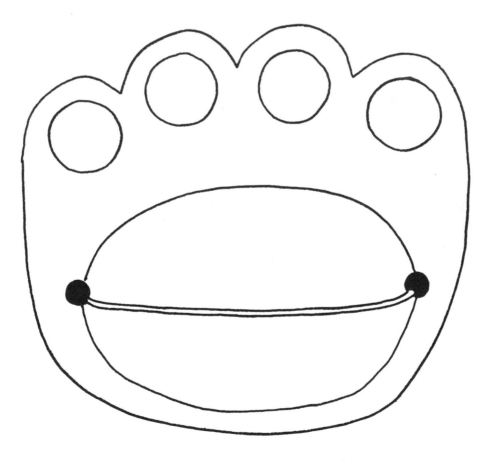

Figure F

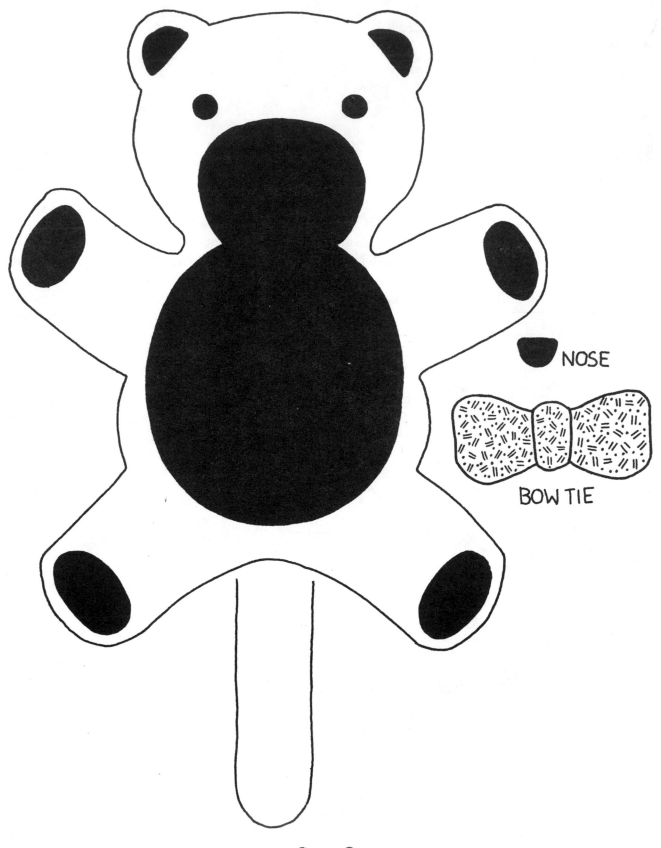

NOSE

BOW TIE

Figure G

Bear Stick Puppets

A simple bear stick puppet is a perfect vehicle for a young child's dramatic play.

Materials: Brown poster board (1 sheet for 9 puppets); tongue depressors; glue; brown, black, and 2 other contrasting colors of felt.

To make the pattern: Trace the outline of the bear, nose, stomach, bow tie, 1 paw pad, and 1 ear pad separately (6 pieces) in Figure G; cut out. Transfer the cutout patterns onto cardboard, drawing along the outline; cut out. Use the cardboard pieces as templates for making the bear stick puppets.

For each stick puppet: Trace the outline of the bear, using the bear template, on brown poster board; cut out. Glue the poster-board bear to a piece of brown felt measuring 7 x 8 inches; let dry. Trim the felt to the edges of the poster-board bear. Pin the patterns for the paw pads (cut 4), ear pads (cut 2), and stomach to a single color of felt (not brown); cut out. Glue these details to the felt side of the brown bear according to Figure G. Following Figure G, cut a nose and eyes from black felt, glue to the bear; let dry. Pin the bow tie pattern to a second color of felt; cut out and glue to the bear. Glue the tongue depressor to the back of the bear (see Figure G) and weight the puppet down with a book while allowing to dry. Make sure that the weight is distributed evenly so that the bear does not pop off the stick while drying.

Alternative: Eliminate the use of felt; use construction paper details glued directly to the poster-board bear form for a completely paper version of the puppet.

Two-Story Bear House

Here is an inexpensive, dramatic party prop that will endlessly amuse very young children. It is well worth the time and effort to make this house. The construction is extremely straightforward (see Figure H), but somehow the addition of the second level and decorations make it seem wildly exciting to children.

When this bear house is used in a party, hide it until you want the children to play in it. Put the box in a remote corner of the room and cover it with a sheet(s) or leave it in a separate room until needed.

Materials: Box from a refrigerator (or other large appliance); a smaller packing box; packing tape; rolls of brown wrapping paper; brown poster board; doilies or Con-Tact paper for scallop decoration, green marker, construction paper for tulips, and tape (optional).

To make the house: (1) Turn the refrigerator box on its side, leaving one end open and the other closed. This adds to the stability of the box. (2) Take the small packing box and cut the end flaps off of what will be the top and the long side flaps off of what will be the bottom. Be careful! This should leave the top with long flaps and the bottom with short flaps. (3) Center the small packing box on the top of the refrigerator box—bottom down, top up—the way it will appear in the finished state. With a pencil, trace around the bottom of the smaller box, flaps tucked in, on the top of the refrigerator box. (4) Cut 1–2 inches inside these lines to form a hole in the top of the refrigerator box (the hole should be slightly smaller than the outline of the packing box). (5) Cut a window in the front side of the smaller packing box. (6) Completely wrap the sides of the smaller box (covering the window) with a sheet of brown wrapping paper folded to the height of the box. DO NOT cover the bottom or top of the box. Secure the sheet of paper with tape. Feel to find the window. Puncture a hole in the paper at the center of the window. Carefully cut from the center, diagonally, to all 4 corners of the window. Fold the triangles of paper to the insides of the window, trim, and secure with tape to finish off the window opening. (7) Center the bottom of the smaller box (end flaps extended outward) over the hole in the top of the refrigerator box. Keeping the box in this position, tape the end flaps to the top of the refrigerator box to secure the second story in place. (8) Cover the entire big box with wrapping paper, leaving the entrance open. Securely tape in place. (9) Deco-

rate the large box along the upper edge with doilies to form a scallop, or a scallop cut from white Con-Tact paper, and with tulips cut from construction paper along the lower edge. Draw the stems directly on the paper with a green marker. (10) To make the roof, first fold 2 (or more as required) sheets of poster board in half. Position them atop the second story to complete a roof. Tape them together and then secure them in place by reaching inside to tape the long side flaps to the inside of the roof.

The minute the first child walks into this house and realizes that he or she can peek out the upper window, or even just throw a bear out, you will be confident that this project represents time well spent.

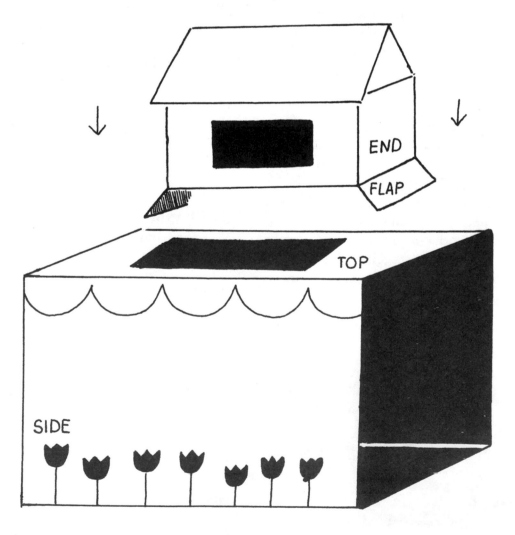

Figure H

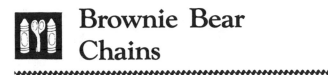

Brownie Bear Chains

A paper doll chain is fascinating to children. Here it is transformed into a bear chain, used first as a party wall decoration and then in a coloring project. Whether the chain is large or small, children are excited by the presentation, making coloring infinitely more engaging.

Materials: Brown wrapping paper; ruler; paper clips; chalk or crayons; construction paper.

To make the pattern: Draw a single bear according to Figure I, enlarging the pattern so that the height of the bear is 4–6 inches less than the width of the wrapping paper; cut out. Note that the ends of a leg and arm on each side are in a straight vertical line.

To make the chain: Trace a single bear squarely on the end of a roll of brown wrapping paper, with the head (top) and feet (bottom) along the long edges of the roll. Rule off a straight line from the top to bottom along the edges of the arm and leg on the raw end of the paper; cut along this

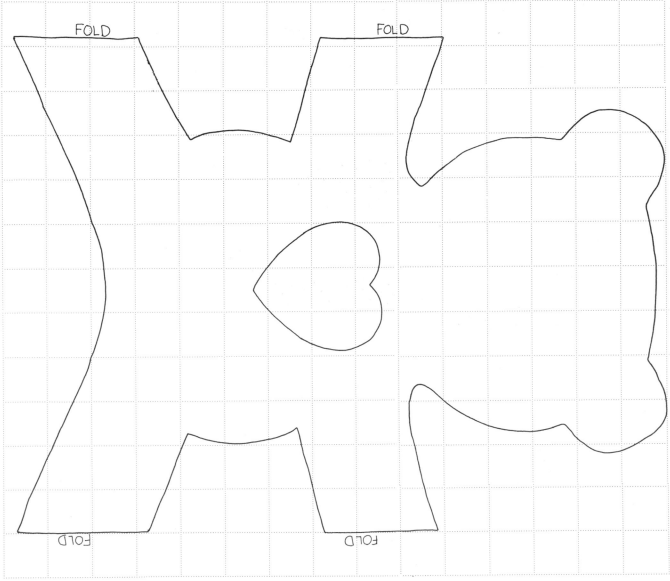

FOLD   FOLD

FOLD   FOLD

Figure I

Figure J

line. Fold the paper along the edges of the opposite arm and leg so that the width of the piece from the edge to the fold is precisely the width of the bear. Continue to fold the paper accordion-fashion, to this width, for at least as many bears as there are children attending the party. Paper clip the folded edges of the stack as well as the top and bottom, to keep the paper from slipping. Cut along the solid outlines of the bear. Unfold the chain, 1 bear at a time, and decorate each with a construction paper heart. Hanging the chain in one piece may not be possible if your walls are not long enough or if there are lots of children. In this case, segment the chain before hanging it—with as many bears as possible in each chain. Hand the children the chalk or crayons and cut single bears off the chain for them to color.

Alternative: Following Figure J, trace a single bear pattern for a smaller bear chain. Cut out a 6–8 bear chain for each child and several extras for decorating the walls. Each child is then given his or her own bear chain to decorate when the project begins.

 Awards Ceremony

Award sticker medallions to the bears that children bring to the party; fresh ribbons for neckties will be graciously received by all the guests, too. Announce the "most huggable," "cuddliest," "most distinguished," "best dressed," "biggest," "fuzziest," "smallest," "handsomest," "prettiest," "most adorable," "softest," etc., and applaud each bear. You'll make both the children and bears feel very special.

Bear Box

This box is intended to be used as a party-favor box, containing goodies to be shared by children with their bears. Neckties, candies, stickers, honeycomb necklaces made from yellow-painted wagon-wheel macaroni, and other small items fit neatly into this container.

Materials: Colored poster board; tape; construction paper; felt-tip pen.

To make the pattern: Draw a pattern according to Figure K on heavy paper. The pattern should include a solid outline for cutting and hash marks at the inside edges for fold lines. Cut out.

For each box: Trace the outline of the box, using the pattern, on poster board, reproducing all solid lines and hash marks for fold lines; cut along all solid lines. Crease the form on every fold line. Cut the slot in the roof according to the pattern. To assemble, lift one side and one

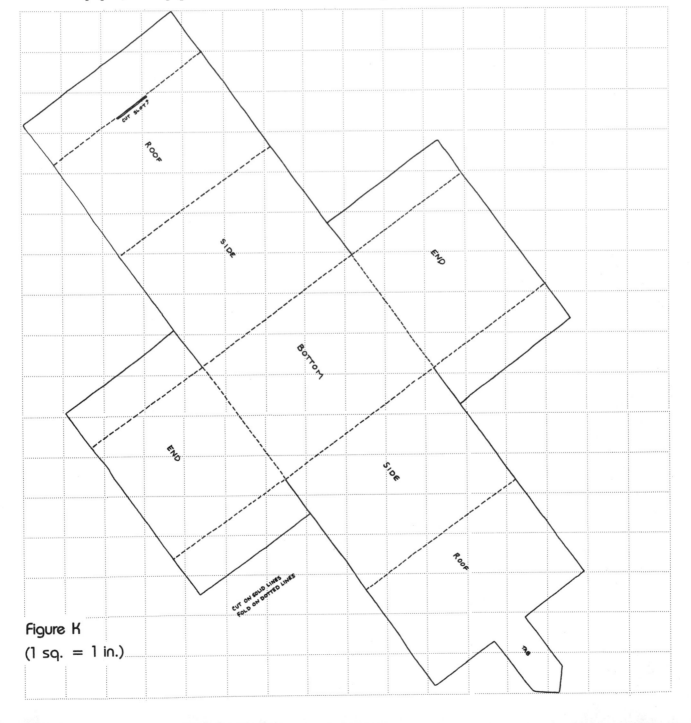

CUT SLOT?

ROOF

SIDE

END

BOTTOM

END

SIDE

ROOF

CUT ON SOLID LINES
FOLD ON DOTTED LINES

Figure K
(1 sq. = 1 in.)

end up until they meet, tucking the extra allowance along the end section inside the side. Tape together on the inside so that the side and end section are flush and at right angles. Repeat this until the square bottom of the box is constructed, always taping the box securely on the inside. Insert the tab in the roof slot to complete the structure. Decorate the sides of the box with construction paper hearts and each child's name (see Figure L). This box will become the perfect container for bear paraphernalia.

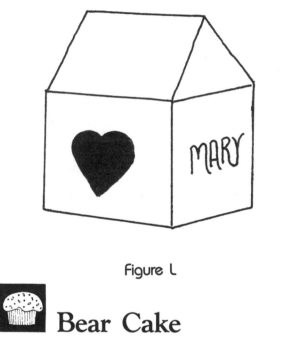

Figure L

Bear Cake

A simple 9 x 13-inch chocolate sheet cake, transformed into a bear, will be a hit at the party.

Materials: One 9 x 13-inch cake (see Cake Tips in "How to Use This Book"); 1 can or batch of chocolate icing; 1 can or small batch of white icing mixed with red food coloring; red shoestring licorice; peanut butter chips; 3 black jelly beans; chocolate jimmies (sprinkles).

To finish the cake: Following the pattern in Figure M, draw a full-size pattern (8 x 12 inches) for the bear base and 2 heart pieces; cut out. Lay the pattern pieces directly on the cake and cut

along the edges with a sharp, large knife, keeping it as vertical as possible when cutting. Frost the bear top and sides with chocolate icing. Referring to Figure N, fill in the ear rounds, paw pads, and mask of the bear with peanut butter chips. Add a black jelly bean on its side for the nose and 2 black jelly beans poked into the cake on end for the eyes. Dust the uncovered part of the cake with chocolate jimmies (sprinkles) to resemble fur. Assemble the heart separately, sticking the 2 pieces together with pink icing; frost the outside top and sides with pink icing. Carefully lift the heart up on a spatula and slide it into place on the bear's body. Tie several strands of red shoestring licorice into a bow. Trim the ends to the desired length and place on the bear's neck.

Suggestions

This cuddly party is ideally a short luncheon party. Children's bears should be given name tags upon arrival to avoid confusion or loss. Remind Mom or Dad to keep track of the bears and encourage them to participate in all the events of the party. Extra bears borrowed from much older friends or siblings should be LOANED to children who have forgotten to bring a bear. It's a good idea also to remind parents of the bring-along component when they R.S.V.P.; this will lessen the likelihood of their forgetting the bear.

There is no animal or theme so thoroughly commercially exploited as the bear. This makes buying or renting accessories for this party—including favors—quite simple. Bear videotapes, books, coloring books, stickers, stuffed animals, toys—the full array of entertainment, activities, toys, and useful items decorated with pictures of bears (toothbrushes, mugs, adhesive bandages, washcloths, ribbons, stationery, etc.) can be bought as substitutions or favors for this party. The wonder of children at this age is that they will say excitedly, "MORE bears!" rather than groan "more bears?" So, ham it up and get some more bears!

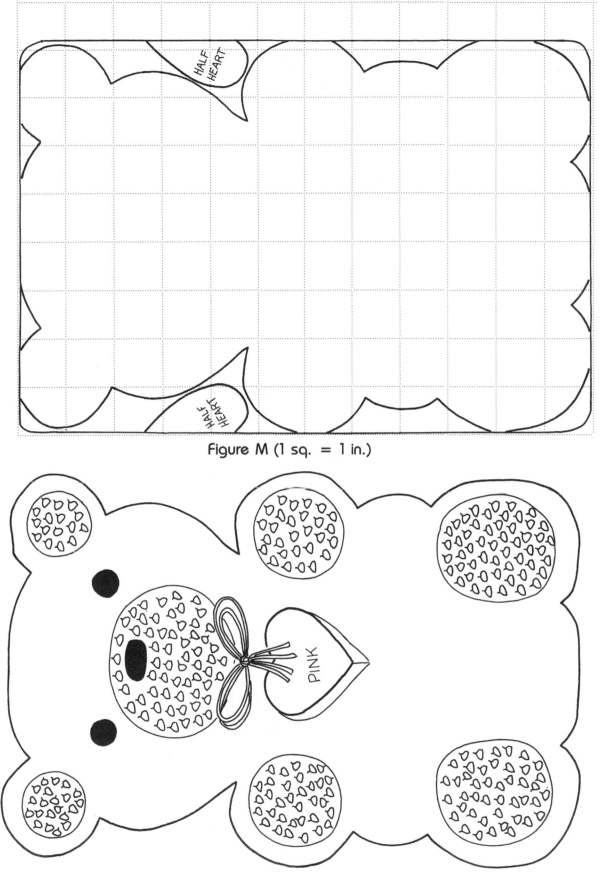

HALF HEART

HALF HEART

Figure M (1 sq. = 1 in.)

PINK

Figure N

2

TRAFFIC JAM

```
┌─────────────────────────────┐
│         AGE GROUP           │
│       3 to 4 years old      │
│                             │
│        PARTY LENGTH         │
│        1 to 1½ hours        │
└─────────────────────────────┘
```

Creating the illusion of highways and byways will engage children and parents in this bring-along car party designed for the very young. For children with a car fixation, this party is a dream come true.

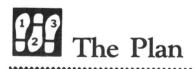 The Plan

A Car-and-Map Invitation announces the event, asking children to bring a matchbox car and Mom or Dad to the party. A map that shows a series of obvious landmarks to help the children "find their way to the party" is enclosed. Playing this location game on the way to your house will put both child and parent in a true car mood.

The party is already in motion when the guests arrive. Have parents label the children's bring-along cars with name tags while children hunt for felt cars hidden around the room(s). These cars will be used later as part of an art project. As the hunt winds down, give the children a chance to direct traffic with a game of Stop and Go. Racing down lanes of kid-sized roads, demarcated with tape on the floor, children (and parents) watch attentively as they try to zoom and stop to the signals of the leader. When this game

16

is over, set up a Road Test, a series of physical challenges in the form of an obstacle course that will further test the children's skill and concentration. At this point, a pit stop is in order. Lead the group to refreshments by following a trail of Arrows stuck on the wall.

At the table, have children don their Bumper-to-Bumper Traffic Headbands as you bring out the cake. Singing a favorite car or bus song will diminish their impatience while you serve the Car Cake. Have the children work on a sit-down project with Felt Boards and roadside scenery following refreshments; this will extend the "quiet time." Children will arrange and rearrange their felt pieces endlessly, pausing only to admire their friends' art.

During the Felt Board project, transform the main party room into car heaven by setting up the Racing Ramps and Road Network, scaled to the matchbox cars. Add Road Signs, if desired. Racing cars down the ramps to a crashing end, threading them through tunnels, and sending them over and under bridges will easily entertain both parents and children for the remainder of the party. Finally, give each child a ramp or road segment and a road sign to take home. With party favors and treats in hand, children leave feeling that they have had a birthday special. After the last child is gone, the birthday child will be thrilled to open presents and extend the event with the family.

Mapping Out the Birthday

A minimap tucked into a car-shaped pouch delivers the message that will get the party wheels rolling. The map is designed so that, with a bit of help, even a 3 year old can try to navigate the distance between home and the party.

Materials: Red or blue poster board (1 sheet for 12 invitations); white and blue or red Con-Tact paper (or construction paper); tracing paper or other white paper (for the map); pipe cleaners; double-stick tape; ballpoint or felt-tip pen; envelopes.

To make the pattern: Trace the outline of the double car shown in Figure A on paper; cut out. Trace the wheel and hubcap on the single car shown in Figure B; cut out. Transfer the cutout patterns onto cardboard, drawing along the outline; cut out. Use these cardboard pieces as the templates for making the invitations.

For each invitation: To make the pouch, trace around the edges of the double-car template on red or blue poster board; cut out. Crease along the fold line to create a 2-sided single car; close using double-stick tape in the areas indicated in Figure A. DO NOT put any tape in the center section of the car. Trace 4 wheels on white Con-Tact paper using the template; cut out. Trace 4 hubcaps on red or blue Con-Tact paper using the template; cut out. Stick the hubcaps on the wheels. Stick the wheels on the car, 2 on the front and 2 on the back, matching the front and back sides, to look like the wheels in Figure B. To make the map, cut a 4- or 5-inch square of tracing or other paper. Using a ballpoint or felt-tip pen, draw a few roads and 2 or 3 major landmarks between your home and the individual guest's home, or confine the landmarks to those very near your home that all the guests must pass on their way. (Major landmarks should be major to a child and not necessarily major to you. Such things are giant rocks, bridges, staircases, burger stands, schoolhouses, and playgrounds.) Examples are shown in Figure C. Write the invitation information on the map, including a reminder to bring a parent and car to the party and instructions on how to use the map. Fold the map up and insert it into the pouch. Stick a half piece of pipe cleaner in the pouch and tape in place. This antenna will draw attention to the map in the pouch.

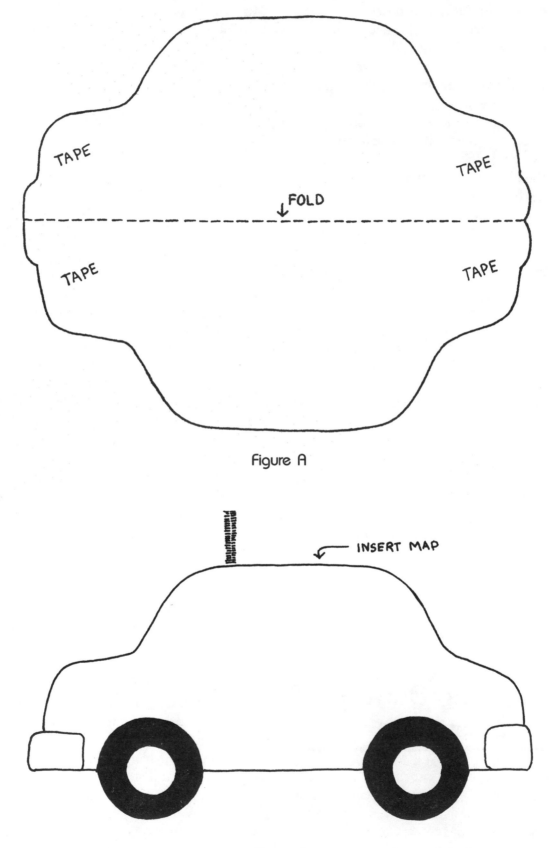

Figure A

Figure B

Text: Race over to (child's name)'s/for a birth-day party!/Date, Time, Place/Bring a matchbox car and Mom or Dad/R.S.V.P./Use this map to help find your way to the party!

Alternatives: Use road signs made according to the directions in this chapter and write invitation text on the back.

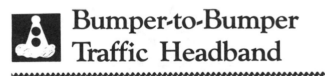

Figure C

Bumper-to-Bumper Traffic Headband

This sweet and easy headband for youngsters uses 1 car to tie up traffic!

Materials: Red and yellow poster board (1 sheet of each for 25 bands); blue and metallic Con-Tact papers; double-stick tape; round-cord elastic; ruler. (Plain or glossy papers substitute nicely for Con-Tact papers here.)

To make the pattern: Trace the outline of the car set for the headband shown in Figure D on paper; cut out. Trace a wheel and a hubcap from Figure D; cut out. Transfer the cutout patterns onto cardboard, drawing along the outline; cut out. Using a ruler, draw a 1¼ x 12-inch band on cardboard; cut out. Use these cardboard pieces as the templates for the headband.

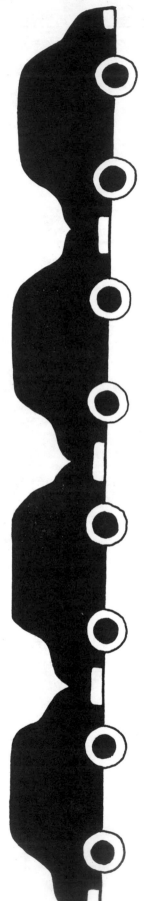

Figure D

For each headband: Trace the outline of the car template on yellow poster board and the band template on red poster board; cut out. Using the templates, trace and cut out 8 wheels in blue Con-Tact paper and 8 hubcaps in metallic Con-Tact paper. Stick the metallic hubcaps on the wheels and the wheels into position on the cars, according to the headband in Figure D. For the bumpers, cut a narrow strip of metallic Con-Tact paper to the width of the bumpers shown in Figure D, and then snip individual pieces to the length of the individual bumpers shown. Affix the bumpers. Center the cars on the straight red band and attach using double-stick tape. Punch holes at the end of the straight band and tie together with round-cord elastic.

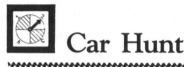

Car Hunt

When the children first arrive, have them race to find the felt cars hidden throughout the party room! The children will add these to their stash of felt pieces for the felt board project—happy to find them and happy to keep them.

To make felt cars: Trace the car drawing in Figure H (see page 24); cut out. Using this as a pattern, pin to scraps of brightly colored felt; cut out.

Stop and Go

Making kid-sized roads by sticking 2 lines of masking tape to the floor 24 inches apart (as long as you can accommodate and as complicated as you can bear to make them) sets the stage for this classic children's game. In one version, an adult starts the music, and children race around on the kid roads; when the adult stops the music, the children freeze. Music should be selected for a variety of tempos, since children will naturally slow down and speed up to the beat of the music. In another version, children are given a chance to be traffic cops, holding up a red paddle to indicate that the children must stop and a green paddle to indicate that they may go. Ping Pong paddles are put to excellent use in this game. Background music adds to the fluid movement of the paddle version as well.

 ## Road Test

Set up simple obstacle courses for the children to run. Human bridges to crawl under (use those spare moms and pops), blocks to hop over and weave around, and lines to walk on or between are all easy physical challenges for very young children. With adult supervision, the experience will be safe and fun.

 ## Ramp Races

Arrange racing ramps in one location or a series of kid slides funneling into a central area to allow the children to race their cars in a continuous fashion. The cars will achieve a certain speed, and if the racing ramps are put on a table, the cars will crash to a landing, lending an innocent daredevil thrill to the proceedings. Either the quieter race or the more raucous crash ending will keep the children and adults very busy.

Racing ramps decorated with colorful tunnels make wonderful party props and favors. These ramps seem wildly unusual and fun to the children and are perfect for racing tiny cars.

Materials: A strip of corrugated cardboard taken from the side of a box, roughly 3–4 feet long and 6–9 inches wide; poster board; cellophane or streamers; packing tape and tape; white and black Con-Tact paper or white and black children's poster paint.

To make each ramp: Bend the strip of corrugated cardboard to the shape shown in Figure E.

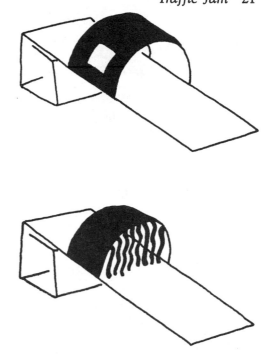

Figure E

The height of the ramp should be roughly 5½ inches. Cut a strip of white Con-Tact paper 2 inches wider than the width of the cardboard and 2 inches longer. Tape the ramp into the finished position, taping underneath (inside the end piece that wraps around). To stick the Con-Tact paper on the ramp, begin at the bottom. Peel off the backing to the length of the slide portion of the ramp and center on the ramp, leaving an extra 1 inch on the bottom and side edges. Wrap the excess inch around the edges and miter the corners. Peeling off the backing, follow the ramp around, sticking on Con-Tact paper and wrapping around the edges to finish, clipping at corners and bends to miter. Add black centerline markers—2 narrow strips of black Con-Tact paper. To make the tunnel, cut a strip of poster board 5 inches wide. The length of this strip will depend on the width of the ramp. A 9-inch-wide ramp takes a strip roughly 23 inches long. With packing tape, attach the strip to form the tunnel shown in Figure E, taping it underneath the ramp to avoid creating ridges. Add streamers or cellophane strips to the upper edge of the tunnel, taping in place.

The Road Network

This is the party's major prop—a maze of roads suitable for toy cars to run on. Tunnels, ramps, bridges, signs, and crossroads are all a challenge to the young driver.

Materials: Packing boxes (*same* size) cut down into 4 smooth sides, without the flaps; Con-Tact papers; miscellaneous small gift boxes, oatmeal boxes, shoe boxes, etc.—any box made of strong cardboard; Styrofoam (optional); packing tape.

To make pieces for the road segment: Make a road base by covering cut-down box side with a sheet of solid-color Con-Tact paper. The road (3–4-inch-wide strips of yellow or black Con-Tact paper), and an obstacle will be added to the top of each base to make a road segment (see Figure F). Select a container to use on this road segment. Each segment should have 1 obstacle or challenge. Suggestions for treatment of the containers include: cutting bottom off an oatmeal box and covering the outside with Con-Tact paper to create a tunnel; cutting archways in opposite sides of a box to create a bridge underpass; cutting a shoe box down to make a ramp. Make the shoe-box ramp by cutting slits from the top to the bottom at the 4 corners of the shoe box. Then cut off half the height from the long sides of the shoe box. Cut a piece of Styrofoam to fit under the rectangular portion of the shoe box, leaving the ends free and the top stable, or staple strips to hold the shortened long sides in place. Turn the box over; the ends become the ramp sections, and the bottom the overpass; cover this surface with Con-Tact paper (see Figure G). To make roads, cut long strips (the length of the cardboard base plus 2 inches to wrap around the ends of the segment) of yellow or black Con-Tact paper 3⅜ inches wide.

To assemble individual road segments: When laying the road on the road segment, make sure that the roads are an equal distance from

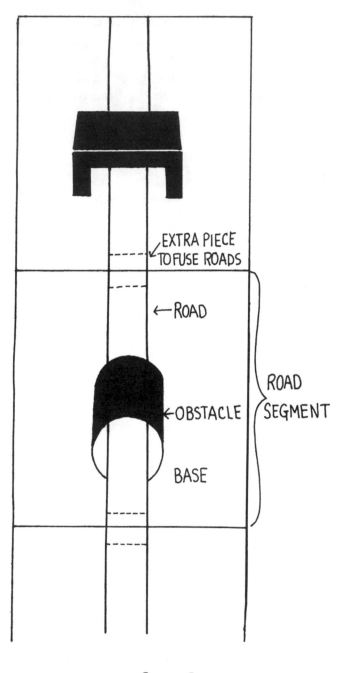

Figure F

the edge of the board base on all the segments. Attach the obstacle or container to the road segment so that this evenness of road is maintained. Use a strong packing tape. In some cases, you lay Con-Tact paper road strips before the obstacle is attached; in some cases, you must attach the obstacle first. For example, lay roads going under box bridges first, then tape the bridges into place; on the other hand, attach an oatmeal container

Figure G

tunnel first and then put the road through the tunnel and reinforce the attachment. (Carefully fused poster-board roads can be substituted for the Con-Tact paper roads and attached with strong tape.)

Road network assembly: Because the road network is segmented, it can be easily stored before the party and, with advance preparation, quickly assembled while the party is in progress. Make a plan in advance that shows where the segments will be placed and how they will fit together. Precut short segments of Con-Tact paper roads to place over the edges of the segments and join them together. These joiners can be removed after the play is over, and the road segments given away as party favors. If you intend to use them as favors, you must make as many segments as there are children invited to the party.

Alternatives: Commercially available plastic road-and-town mats can be the scenery for this part of the party. Borrowing extras from other car fanatics will increase the pleasure since all the children will be able to play at the same time.

About-Town Felt Board

Here is a manageable project for both children and parents that creates a quiet, picturesque moment in this party. A felt board with simple felt shapes that add up to a roadside scene will give each child a sense of accomplishment. It's also a terrific take-home party favor.

Materials: White or blue felt (1 yard for every 12 boards); yellow felt; smaller pieces of other colors of felt; glue; stiff cardboard; small bags.

To make patterns: Following the drawings in Figure H, make paper patterns for all the shapes shown; cut out. These patterns are scaled to be used with a cardboard base measuring 18 x 12 inches. The base can be any size; however, the scale of the shapes must be roughly preserved.

For each felt board: Cover a stiff piece of 18 x 12-inch cardboard (or smoothly cut corrugated cardboard) with white or blue felt; glue in place and trim the edges of the felt to the edges of the board. Cut an 18 x 4-inch strip of yellow felt for the road on the felt board; lay it in place at the bottom. Make 1 for each child. Pinning paper patterns to felt, cut shapes from contrasting colors. Be sure to cut plenty of pieces for each child.

For each child: Present the felt board along with a bag of felt pieces at a table or on the floor. Encourage parents to get the child going on the project. Since felt sticks to felt, pictures can be arranged and rearranged, and stick without using an adhesive.

Figure H

 Road Signs

Simple, craft-stick road signs are fun additions to little roads and great party favors.

Materials: Red, yellow, black, white, and blue poster board or poster board covered with papers in these colors (use scrap pieces of poster board from other projects and whole sheets); double-stick tape; craft sticks; clay.

To make patterns: Trace individual shapes (do not trace the craft sticks, only the geometrical shapes) shown in Figure I; cut out. Transfer the cutout patterns onto cardboard, drawing along the outlines; cut out. Use these cardboard pieces as the templates for the road signs.

To make signs: These signs merely suggest actual road signs in color and shape. Because of this, the color choice is important; lettering can be added if it seems desirable to you. The octagon is traced on red poster board, the vertical rectangle

Figure I

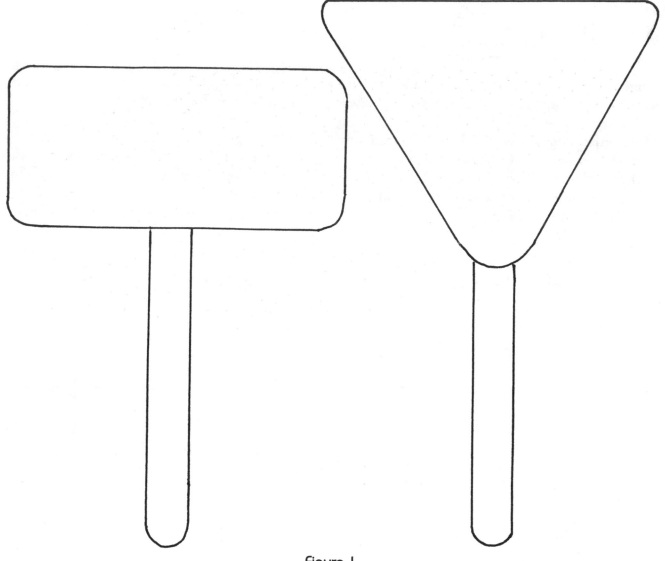

Figure I

on white and blue poster board, the horizontal rectangle on black poster board, and the triangle on yellow poster board. Each sign requires a front and back, so cut 2 shapes for each sign. Trace the templates of the sign shapes on poster board and cut 2 for each sign. To assemble the sign, attach double-stick tape to the top 1 inch of the craft stick on both sides; sandwich it between the front and back sign pieces. With additional double-stick tape, press the edges of the front and back of the sign together. (This can all be done with glue.) If you feel compelled to letter the sign, do so *before* assembling. To post the sign, stick the bottom of the craft stick in a lump of clay!

Arrows and the Car Cake

Following a complicated series of arrows on the wall leading to the car cake will increase interest in the refreshments. The arrow pattern is shown in Figure J. The cake at the end of the road is a simple car cake. Any road sign design can be used for the cake as well.

Materials for the car cake: A 9 x 13-inch sheet cake (see Cake Tips in "How to Use This Book"); 1 can or batch of white frosting; green

Figure J

and blue food colors; round fruit-flavored candies such as Skittles, or chocolate candies like M & M's.

To finish the cake: Following the pattern in Figure K (see page 28), draw full-size patterns for the car body, bumpers (2), and wheels (2) on paper; cut out. Lay the pattern pieces directly on the cake and cut along the edges with a sharp, large knife, keeping it as vertical as possible when cutting. Ice the sides of the bumpers and wheels that will connect to the body of the car and stick the pieces in place to assemble the cake according to Figure L (see page 28). Tint small amounts of icing green and blue. Ice the wheels in blue and the windows in green, following Figure L. Cover the remainder of the cake top and sides with white icing. Add red candies to form the hubcap. For a more even appearance, edge the wheels with red candies and the windows with green candies stuck in vertically. Create front headlights with yellow candies and rear taillights with red candies.

Suggestions

This is ideally a very short party with a strong emphasis on free play. Nevertheless, play should directly involve the adults; parents must be encouraged to participate. And be sure to have extra cars on hand for children who forget to bring them.

If and when the party is given in warm weather, a parade of riding toys, decorated and brought to the party, may be substituted for another activity.

In general, car products are very easy to find and often inexpensive. Car-imprinted paper products are always available. Small cars, boxes to store cars in (marked in durable ink—"car box"), postcards picturing antique cars, coloring books, storybooks, and so on are all favors that children will enjoy for a long time.

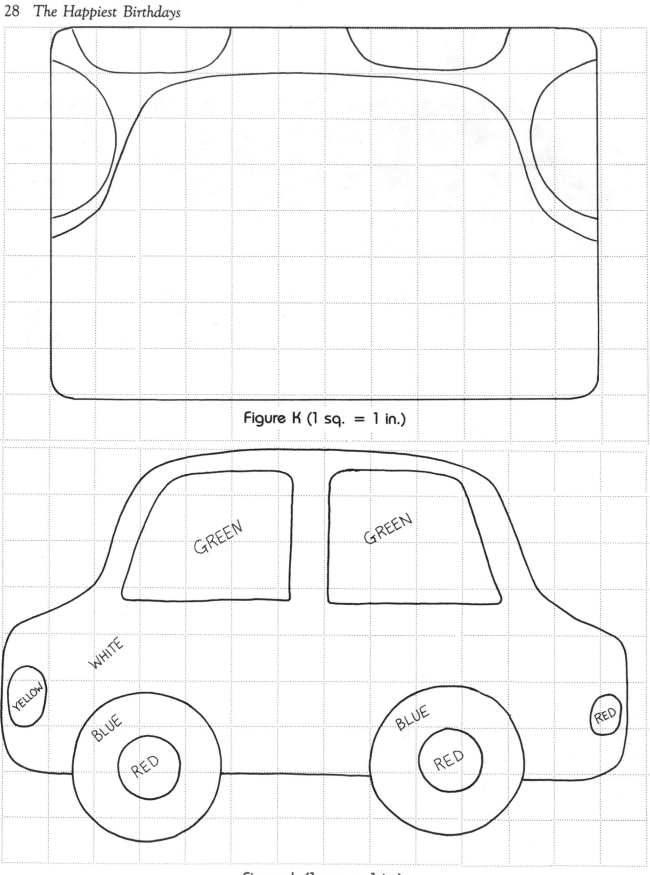

Figure K (1 sq. = 1 in.)

Figure L (1 sq. = 1 in.)

3

BUMBLEBEES AND BUTTERFLIES

Butterflies and bumblebees capture the hearts of the young as soon as they pass within sight. Flying through the air, dressed in colorful regalia, they're nature's mobile for young eyes. Here's a party that takes children on a short flight into fantasy—capitalizing on bees and butterflies all the way!

 The Plan

Send an invitation that will get this party off to a flying start—deliver the birthday message

on the wings of a paper Butterfly Puppet. It comes with an assortment of colorful paper or felt shapes, sequins, and other fancy bits, which the child can use to decorate his/her own butterfly. When completed, the butterfly slips onto the child's hand via an elastic band, and with the flick of the wrist, the butterfly "takes flight." On the day of the party, each child brings his/her puppet along to take part in a Butterfly "Pet" Show.

Begin the party itself by having the children search for the Bee's Nest—a goody-filled paper bag that opens up with the pull of a ribbon. "Bumble" Puppets, clutched in the children's hands, add to the merriment of this search. After a few rounds of Buzz, Buzz, Bee, have the children fly off to the project table, which is set with slip-on Butterfly Wings (simple poster board cutouts) decorative goodies (e.g., streamers, curly ribbons, sequins, beads, feathers, etc.), and glue. The children may decorate the wings to their hearts' content, creating their own special "costumes." While the glue dries, have the children gather together and "show" their butterflies. Award them all for their winning entries with Butterfly Motion Hats. Seat them once again at the table and sing a round of the birthday song. With butterfly hats moving to every note, bring in the Butterwiches and Bumblewiches, and then the *pièce de résistance*, a decorated Butterfly Cake, which will be quickly gobbled up.

When their feasting is finished and energy renewed, have the children leave the table, put on their decorated wings, and play Follow the Leader, simulating the sounds and motions of bees and butterflies, moving and dancing for as long as they wish. What a colorful extravaganza! They can play a quick game of Catch the Queen Bee before dispersing to their natural homes with their hats, wings, and Bee's Nest goodies in hand.

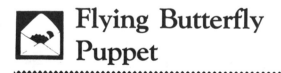 Flying Butterfly Puppet

The flying butterfly takes off to deliver the birthday message and soon becomes a constant companion of the party goer. Donning an elastic "leash," flappable wings, and lots of decorative goodies, she really has what it takes to provide a lot of entertainment. And she's easy to make!

Materials: Colorful poster board (one sheet for every 6 butterflies); colorful construction paper and/or felt pieces; sequins (optional); small plastic wiggle eyes (2 for each butterfly); fuzzy pipe cleaners; glue; hole puncher; round-cord elastic; small, plastic lunch bags; white paper; envelopes; felt-tip marker.

To make the pattern: Draw the outline of the butterfly as shown in Figure A on cardboard; cut out. Use this piece as the template for making the butterflies.

For each invitation: Trace the template on poster board; cut out. With a marker, draw the head only on a piece of colorful paper or felt; cut out. Glue the paper/felt onto the butterfly head. (You can also do this for the body.) Glue on the eyes; then make 2 holes, using the hole puncher, right above the eyes. Stick a halved piece of pipe cleaner through the holes to form the antennae (see Figure A). Write the birthday information on a piece of paper cut to fit the "body" of the butterfly; secure loosely with glue for easy removal later on. Make 2 small punch holes in the middle of the body, being sure not to cut off the text; lace an 8-inch piece of round-cord elastic through and tie it on the wrong side to form a "leash" for wearing and flying the butterfly.

Then cut at least ten ½- to 1-inch shapes—circles, triangles, hearts, squiggles, V's, etc.—out of colorful paper and/or felt scraps. Place these and some colorful sequins in a plastic bag or small envelope with instructions to decorate the butterfly. Add a reminder to bring the puppet to the party for the Butterfly Show and a note about slipping the elastic band onto the wrist to achieve the best flight without losing the butterfly!

Text: Fly on over to (child's name)'s birthday party!/Decorate me, slip me on your wrist, and bring me along, too! We'll have a Butterfly Pet Show/Date, Time, Place, R.S.V.P./*Reminder*: Don't forget your butterfly!

Alternatives: A simpler version of a flying invitation comes in the form of a construction-paper butterfly, traced as above and secured at the body to a tongue depressor. The children can decorate it with their own markers and crayons.

FLY ON OVER TO ELIZA'S FOR A BIRTHDAY PARTY!
SATURDAY MAY 1ST 12:00-1:30 88 TULIP LANE
RSVP

Figure A (1 sq. = 1 in.)

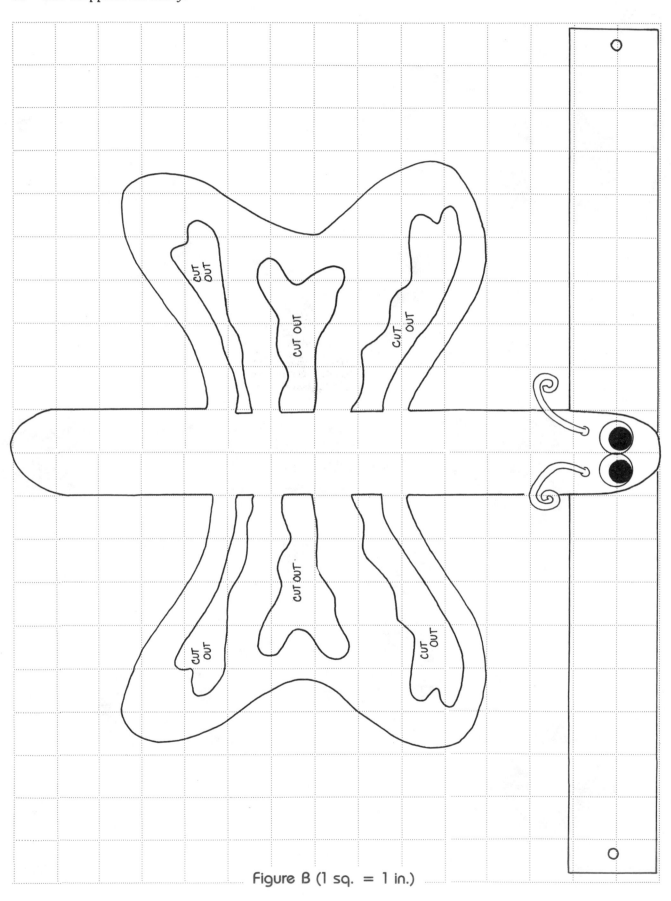

CUT OUT

CUT OUT

CUT OUT

CUT OUT

CUT OUT

CUT OUT

Figure B (1 sq. = 1 in.)

Butterfly Motion Hat

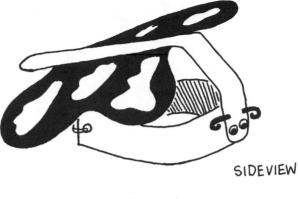

SIDE VIEW

Figure C

These charmingly flappable hats will certainly send spirits soaring! A wiggle or a nod sets the wings in motion.

Materials: Colorful poster board (1 piece for every 2 hats); Con-Tact paper in a contrasting color; large wiggle eyes; fuzzy pipe cleaners; round-cord elastic; hole puncher.

To make the pattern: Draw the outline of the butterfly band, head, and body shown in Figure B on a large sheet of tracing paper. Using this drawing, trace the outline and the interior lines of the wings, shown in the pattern section at the back of this book, to complete the hat pattern; cut out. On a separate sheet of paper, trace the body section only, including the face; cut out. Transfer the cutout patterns onto cardboard; cut out. Use these cardboard pieces as the templates for making the hats.

For each hat: Trace the hat template on poster board and the body-section template on Con-Tact paper; cut out. Be careful cutting the interior of the wings; be sure to use sharp scissors, preferably small in size, but don't worry if the cuts are not exactly as in the pattern. Lay the hat piece out flat and affix the Con-Tact paper body section to the body section of the hat as shown in Figure B. The Con-Tact paper body adds color and stability to the hat. Glue on the wiggle eyes; then punch 2 holes, about ½ inch apart and slightly above the eyes. Lace a halved piece of pipe cleaner through the holes and "curl" the ends to form the antennae. Punch holes at the ends of the straight band and tie together with a 6-inch piece of round-cord elastic (see Figure C). Try the hat on your child's head for fit and watch the butterfly take flight.

Alternatives: The hat could be as simple as a band of poster board, decorated with colorful stick-on butterflies or black and yellow stripes for bees.

 # Find the Bee's Nest

Convert an ordinary brown paper bag into a goody-filled bee's nest. Hide it and see if the little bees can find it!

Materials: Medium-sized brown paper bag; 2 yards of 1-inch-wide ribbon; candies or other soft goodies of your choice; colorful tissue paper or newsprint; white scrap paper; transparent tape; black and yellow marking pens.

To make the nest: Cut 2 small holes in the bottom of the bag, approximately 1 inch apart; lace 1 yard of ribbon through the holes. Turn the bag right side up and add soft candies or other goodies, plus some colorful tissue paper or newsprint to fill. Tie the bag closed with the remaining piece of ribbon to form a "nest." Draw 2 or 3 bees as shown in Figure D on white paper. Color the bees in with yellow and black marking pens and cut out; tape the bees onto the bag. Now you can hang the finished nest with the untied ribbon, securing it at a level so that the children can just reach the ribbon that's tying in the goodies!

At party time, send the children off in all directions, with their "bumble" puppets (discussed later in the chapter) and name-labeled bags in hand, in search of the bee's nest. The first child to find the nest calls out, "Bumble, bumble!" and all the children run to the nest. The birthday child pulls the bow open, and the candies fall out for all to gather and enjoy. (Have extra candies close by to give to anyone who comes up short.)

 # Buzz, Buzz, Bee

Play this game as you do the traditional game of Duck, Duck, Goose, substituting the words, "Buzz, Buzz, Bee!" If you don't know this game, ask your children how to play.

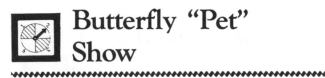 # Butterfly "Pet" Show

All it takes to stage a butterfly "pet" show are some entrants and a judge. The children's decorated invitations fill the first requirement, and you or another adult can be the judge! Gather the children together and give each a chance to "fly" his or her butterfly. Then announce the winners, awarding each child a prize for a different reason (e.g., most colorful, prettiest, best flyer, fastest flyer, etc.). The prize is a butterfly motion hat to fly around in!

> NOTE: Be sure to have some extra butterfly invitations on hand, just in case any of the children forget to bring theirs along. Even without any special decorative additions from the children, these butterflies can win for their fast flying abilities, special flight patterns, great sound effects, etc.!

 # Follow the Leader, Butterfly-Style

The actions and sounds of butterflies and bees are simulated by the "flying" and buzzing children as they follow Mom, Dad, or a helper in and out of rooms and around an obstacle course. This

Figure D

activity is great fun when played with the butterfly motion hats and wings (discussed later). The effect of the colors and motion is incredible.

 ## Catch the Queen Bee

In this game, one child is "It" (the birthday child should be first). He or she counts to 5, and everyone else scatters; then "It" tries to catch the Queen Bee. The child who is caught becomes "It."

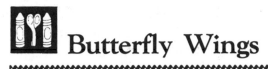 ## Butterfly Wings

These wings may not get the children off the ground, but they will surely get them involved and moving. What's more, they're a lot of fun to make, and most of the making is done by the children! Once decorated, the wings slip onto the children's arms by way of elastic bands.

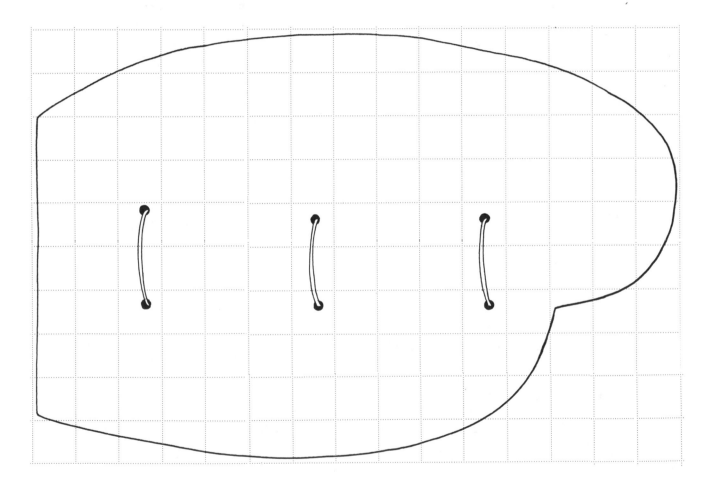

Figure E (1 sq. = 1 in.)

Materials: Poster board (1 sheet for every 2 pairs of wings); hole puncher or awl; round-cord elastic; craft knife; colorful rolls of crepe-paper streamers (you can use 6 different colors for a great rainbow effect); curly ribbon (optional); jumbo sequins, sequins by-the-yard, foil cupcake tins, colorful tissue paper, or any other decorative items you wish to use (glitter, marking pens, stick-on circles, squares, hearts, triangles, stars, etc.); glue; cotton swabs (optional).

To make the pattern: Draw the outline of the pattern on cardboard as shown in Figure E; cut out. Use this piece as the template for making the wings.

For each pair of wings: Trace the template on poster board twice; cut out. Lightly mark the left and right face of the wings. Make 3 pairs of holes in each wing as shown in Figure E, using a hole puncher or awl. Lace an 8-inch piece of elastic through each pair of holes and tie to secure, forming the elastic bands that slide onto the child's arm. Then, using a craft knife, make six 2-inch slashes as shown in Figure F (for weaving through the streamers) and three ¼-inch slashes in each wing for weaving through curly ribbon (optional). Cut 6 pairs of streamers—each a different color,

if desired—ranging in length from 3 to 3½ feet—and 3 pairs of curly ribbon—each several feet long. Lace the streamers through the 2-inch slashes, pulling each piece a little more or a little less than halfway through (to vary the lengths). Do the same with the curly ribbons, pulling them through the ¼-inch slashes and then curling the ends according to manufacturer's instructions.

The wings are now ready to decorate. Gather together the remaining decorative items and prepare a collection on a plate or in a bowl or plastic bag for each child. Have enough glue bottles handy so that there is 1 for every 2 children or prepare a glue pad for each child—a small square of cardboard with a blob of craft glue and a glue stick (a craft stick or cotton swab without the cotton) to spread the glue with. At party time, give each child a set of wings and supplies and explain how to decorate them. Label each pair of wings with its owner's name to avoid confusion at the end of the party.

Alternatives: Instead of adding all the gobbledygook to the cutout wings, have the children color them in to their hearts' content. For a totally fuss-free approach, simply tie streamers on the children's arms and send them soaring.

BACK

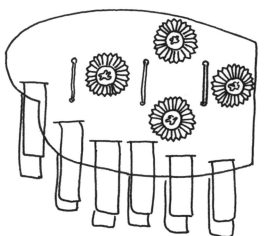

FRONT

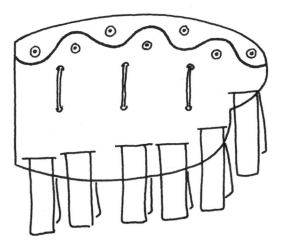

Figure F

"Bumble" Puppets

"Bumble" keeps the party alive long after the last guest has departed. This "bee-witching" puppet is absolutely irresistible.

Materials: Yellow poster board (1 sheet is enough for 6 puppets); black Con-Tact paper; fuzzy pipe cleaners; craft knife; small, plastic wiggle eyes; hole puncher or awl.

To make the pattern: Trace the outline and slashes of the bee puppet on paper as shown in

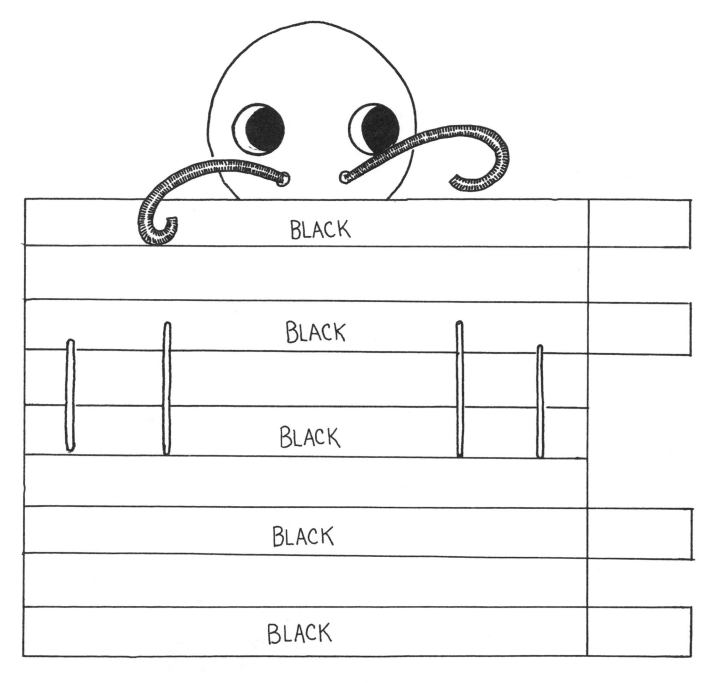

BLACK

BLACK

BLACK

BLACK

BLACK

Figure G

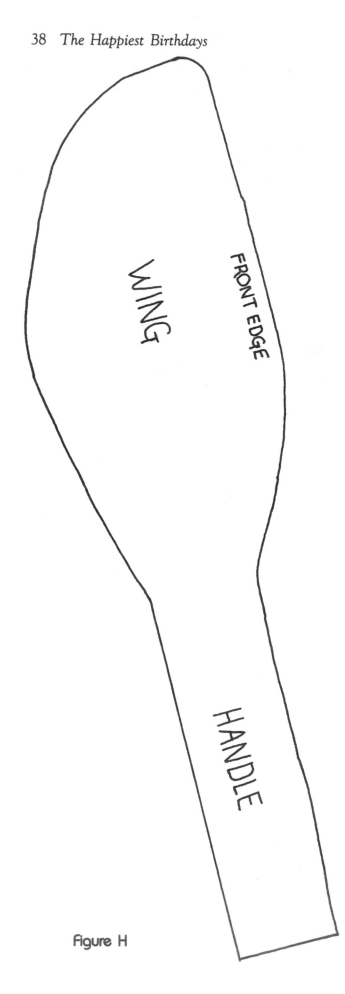

Figure G, eliminating the extended pieces on the side edge, and the wing as shown in Figure H; cut out. Transfer the cutout pattern onto cardboard; cut out. Use these patterns as the templates for making the bee puppets.

To make each puppet: Trace the bee template and 2 wing templates on yellow poster board; cut out. Cut 5 strips of black Con-Tact paper, each ½ x 7 inches. Starting at the back end of the bee's body, affix the black strips to the puppet body as shown in Figure G, overlapping the strips at one end. Using a craft knife, cut the slashes in the body as indicated.

To complete the face, glue on the wiggle eyes and then, using a hole puncher or awl, punch

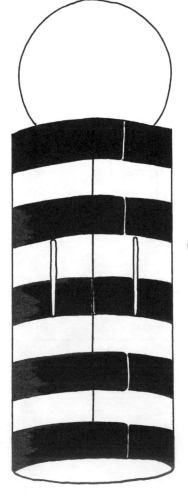

UNDERSIDE
VIEW OF
CONSTRUCTION

figure H

Figure I

2 holes slightly above the eyes and about ½ inch apart. Lace a halved piece of pipe cleaner through the holes to form the antennae. Slip each wing through the slashes so that the bottom of the wing curve is lined up with the inside slash. To complete, curve the body piece so that the lengthwise edges join; secure together with the overlapping Con-Tact paper strips (see Figure I). Gently fold the head down, covering up the front opening. Then, again gently, fold the wings down toward the handle to prepare them for motion.

 # Butterwiches and Bumblewiches

These healthy morsels will fly off the plate and into the mouths in a flash. Simply arrange any sandwich on a plate to resemble a bee or butterfly. As shown in Figure J, one possibility is a sand-wich transformed with the addition of a carrot and 2 apple slices—a luscious butterfly!

 # Butterfly Cake

In keeping with the theme (and not to be up-staged), a simple 9 x 13-inch cake can be transformed into a beautiful butterfly cake.

Materials: One 9 x 13-inch cake (see Cake Tips in "How to Use This Book"); 2 cans or 1½ batches of white or lemon frosting; yellow food coloring (if using white frosting); candies—black licorice laces for the antennae and body definition, licorice logs, lifesavers, jelly beans, and raspberry chews for the rest of the ornamentation.

To finish the cake: Following the pattern in Figure K (see page 40), draw a full-size pattern for the butterfly and cut out. Lay the pattern piece directly on the cake and cut along the edges with a sharp knife, keeping it as vertical as possible when cutting. Frost the top and sides of the cake with yellow frosting and then add the candied details, finishing off with licorice-lace antennae (see Figure L, page 40)!

Suggestions

There are many commercially available products with a butterfly or bee motif that coordinate with this party—bee and butterfly stickers, stationery, stamps, nature books, hair clips, etc. Keep these in mind when buying treats, prizes, or favors and when looking for substitutions for party elements described in this chapter.

- APPLE SLICES

CARROT

Figure J

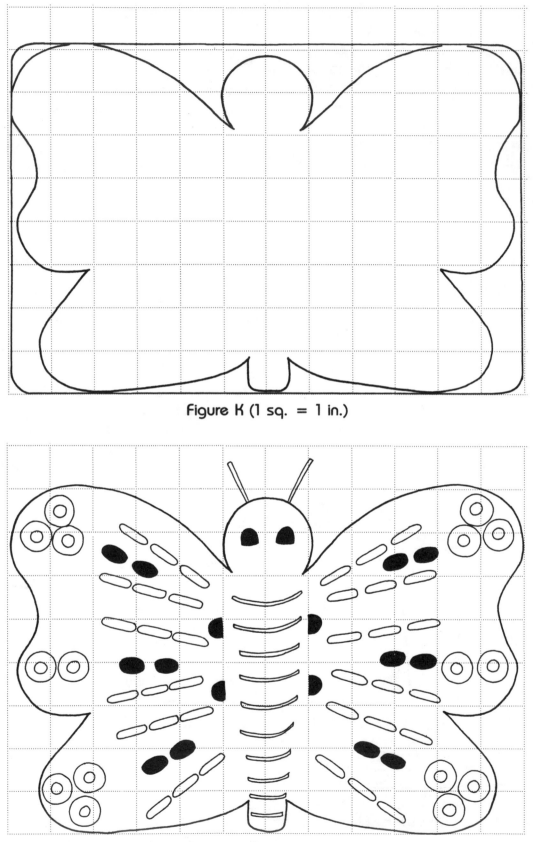

Figure K (1 sq. = 1 in.)

Figure L (1 sq. = 1 in.)

4

MONSTER RUMPUS

AGE GROUP

3 to 5 years old

PARTY LENGTH

1½ hours

Since monsters have been devilified, they have found their way into every corner of children's lives. The Monster Rumpus is a whimsical party based on their happy influence.

 The Plan

And happy are the children who open the mailbox to find a crazy Spinning Monster invitation— a spinner or magnet with so many eyes and the biggest mouth, announcing the birthday party. Toying with this monster will increase the magic of anticipation.

Start off the party with a Hunt for Monster Eggs (packets of jelly beans), and children will busy themselves until all the guests arrive. Then the monster madness begins! Pass out one-half of 2-piece monster-picture puzzles to each child; then have children race to Find Their Better Half. Taken together, the pieces make a funny, loveable face. Seat the guests in a circle and have them play Hot Monster, like Hot Potato, which will challenge them to pass the monster to a neighbor without committing an error.

Wearing Monster Hats, children enjoy monster-like food cut into silly shapes. Simply ask them "who is your favorite monster, and what does it sound like?" and you'll begin a sequence of dramatic monster renditions. The cake is a show stopper, worthy of the biggest and best cake monsters. Everyone will have a "good" piece with all that hair!

After the table is cleared, begin the Make a Monster project. The kids decorate balloons with feet to the point of garishness, using precut materials. They really are quirky and fun. After they name their monsters, have the children set them aside and act out the part. Next, the birthday child can create a Monster Statue Garden, which includes all of his or her friends, who are wearing Monster Sleeves and Monster Hats. Then everyone gets ready for more bounding around in a game of Monster Stomp. With balloons tied to their ankles, the children stomp until they succeed in breaking all the balloons.

For the Monster Story Minute, collect the children in a quiet group for fun and laughter. End the party on a proud, silly note with Monsters on Parade, where children carry large monsters on sticks before the arriving parents and any other onlookers you can round up. When the last monster leaves, the birthday child will be able

to enjoy opening presents in relative peace. Party parents will take this moment to reflect on how sweet monsters can really be!

 # Spinning Monster

A spinning 5-eyed monster in sweat socks sings out the message of the birthday party. This charmer is irresistible!

Materials: Dark blue and white poster board (1 sheet of each for 25 invitations); white, red, and yellow Con-Tact paper; paper clasp; plastic straw; envelopes; 5 plastic eyes (⅜ or ½ inch); hole puncher; glue.

To make pattern: Trace the outline of the monster in Figure A; cut out. Trace the outline of the lips and 4 booties; cut out. Transfer the cutout patterns onto cardboard, drawing along the outline; cut out. Use these cardboard pieces as templates for the invitations.

For each invitation: Using the template, trace a monster outline on blue poster board; cut out. Trace the templates for the booties on white Con-Tact paper and the mouth on red Con-Tact paper; cut out. Attach the booties and mouth to monster. Cut a 4 x ⅛-inch strip of yellow Con-Tact

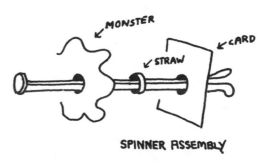

SPINNER ASSEMBLY

Figure A

paper to make the sock tops; snip to fit individual booties, trim, and attach. Affix 5 eyes with glue. To make the card, cut a 4¾ x 3¾-inch square of white poster board. Cut a slit in the middle just large enough to accommodate a paper clasp. On 1 side of the white board, print the invitation text, including instructions for assembling the monster (avoid writing in the center of the card). To make the spinner work, cut a ¼-inch length of straw. With a hole puncher, make a hole in the center of the monster. Take the paper clasp and slip on the monster, then the straw, and finally the card; loosely close the clasp on the back of the card. Spin the monster to make sure it works. If you find the hole is larger than your straw, try a different straw. (Leftover straws from fast-food

outings can be your source. You will need only 1 or 2 for all of the invitations.) Having verified that the invitation is functional, disassemble. Put all 4 elements into the envelope and mail.

Text: Set Me Spinning. (Put me, monster, on the clasp first, then the straw, then the card, and close the clasp in back.)/Now join me in a Monster Rumpus celebrating (child's name)'s birthday/ Date, Time, Place, R.S.V.P.

Alternatives: Make the same invitation using white poster board for the monster and markers to color in the details. Or make the monster segment only and attach a piece of magnetic tape to the back, being careful not to cover the text of the invitation.

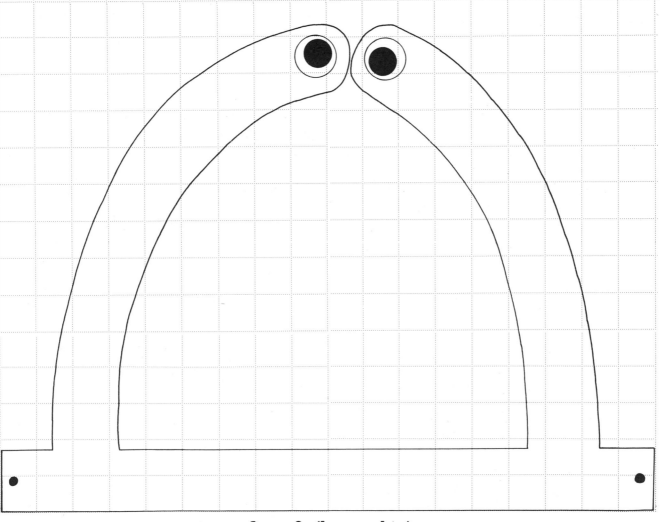

Figure B (1 sq. = 1 in.)

Waggle-eyed Monster Hat

Eyes on tentacles springing from the back of the head transform the wearer into a jiggling, waggle-eyed monster. It couldn't be more fun to wear or easier to make!

Materials: Bright-colored poster board (1 sheet for 2 hats; leftovers can be used for other projects); ¾-inch plastic eyes (2 for 1 hat); round-cord elastic; glue; stapler; hole puncher.

To make the pattern: Draw a full-size pattern, according to the scaled drawing in Figure B (see preceding page), on poster board; cut out. Use the pattern as a template for the monster hats.

For each hat: Using the template, trace around the edges on colored poster board; cut out. Affix the plastic eyes with glue according to Figure B; let dry. Punch holes near the ends of the band as shown in Figure B. The outside (right side) of the band is the same surface as the one the eyes are glued to. Tie the straight band portion closed with round-cord elastic, right side out. Taking the tentacles in hand, cross them over the middle so that the eyes fall towards the front of the band; staple the tentacles together where they cross. See Figure C.

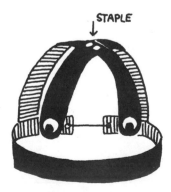

Figure C

Optional: The hat can be decorated further by adding accordion-folded narrow strips of poster board to the spot where it is stapled.

Alternatives: Using the same construction principles, many monsters of a friendly ilk can be created by adding eyelashes, extra eyes, hair, etc. Enjoy!

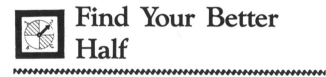

Monster Eggs Everywhere

Do monsters lay eggs? It hardly matters. Kids will endlessly search for small packages of jelly beans even if you don't call them monster eggs, but they will hunt harder if you do. Many packets for each child will infinitely increase the pleasure of the hunt.

Find Your Better Half

This 2-piece puzzle game will send children running from one end of the room to the other, as they speed to piece the monster face together. Cut each monster face in half. Give each child 1 of the 2 pieces. Stick all the possible matches on the wall within reach. The children will find the matching half, then peel their piece off the wall and assemble the puzzle. Each puzzle will surprise a child with a different monster face.

Materials: Corrugated cardboard; poster paint or markers.

To make each puzzle: Copy or create a monster face in pencil on the corrugated cardboard piece (about 11 x 16 inches). Some suggested faces are shown in Figure D. Using bright colors of poster paint, color faces, varying the background

Figure D

colors from puzzle to puzzle. The pictures can be colored broadly with markers instead of paint. When the paint is dry, turn the picture over and draw a jigsawlike line; cut along the line, dividing the picture into 2 pieces. The cutting must be done carefully, since the paint on the other side can chip. Make all the monster puzzles the same size to increase the difficulty of locating the mate and vary the cuts somewhat so that no 2 are alike.

NOTE: When you invent your own monsters, be sure the mood is up and not menacing. The aim here is to entertain, not frighten. Also note that these monster paintings need not be expertly drawn or executed to be effective and fun.

Hot Monster

This game uses a potato decorated with magic markers to look like a monster. Pass the potato around the circle as quickly as possible, from one child to the next. The children are trying to avoid being "burned" by the monster. Dropping the potato stops the game, which is then restarted elsewhere. This game is most appropriate for older (5-year-old) children.

 # Monster Sleeves

Add to the effect of the hats by making textured monster sleeves to be worn as arm cuffs.

Materials: Colored poster board (coordinated or matching the hat); construction papers or poster boards in coordinating colors; double-stick or regular tape; round-cord elastic; hole puncher.

To make a sleeve: Cut out a 4 x 6-inch piece of poster board. (Note first that poster board bends more easily in one direction than the other. Keep this feature in mind when cutting out the sleeves. The sleeves must arc over the arm. The narrow edge of the sleeve should be cut parallel to the long side of the poster board.) Punch 4 holes in the sides according to the placement indicated in Figure E. Cut and decorate 3 strips, 2½ x 4 inches, of contrasting poster board or construction paper (do not mix poster board and construction paper details). Make pleats, curls, etc. following the recommendations in Figure E. Tape the strips on, beginning with the lowest strip pictured and working to the top. Add a round circle at the top of the sleeve for decoration. Tie the sides together with two 6-inch pieces of round-cord elastic, looping and knotting 1 piece through the 2 top holes and the other through the 2 bottom holes. Try it on your own child for an approximate size. It can be adjusted later.

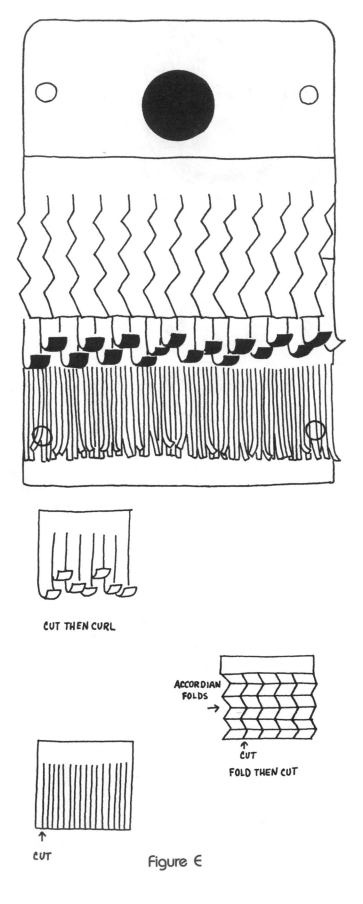

CUT THEN CURL

ACCORDIAN FOLDS →

↑ CUT

FOLD THEN CUT

↑ CUT

Figure E

Monster Statue Garden

Encourage children dressed in full monster regalia to act out monster motions while the birthday child roams the room. When the child taps a monster, he or she must freeze in that position until all the monsters are "still as statues." Other children might like to take a turn as well.

 ## Monster Stomp

Tie a balloon on a ribbon and tie the ribbon around the ankle of each child. A great chase, confusion, and glee will be evidenced as children try to pop each other's ballons. (NOTE: THIS IS NOT A GAME FOR THE TIMID. KNOW YOUR GUESTS. Should the group be at all questionable, substitute another balloon game.)

 ## Monster Story Minute

In this story, children participate in the revelation of Alexi and her (his) personal quirks. Sitting in front of a picture-poster of this monster, children fill in the blanks in a poem describing him or her. A crazy, silly story develops. Add your own verses to the poem to increase the length of the text. The shorter the story, the better, and the more recognizably inappropriate responses are the more fun.

Materials: Sheet of white or brown wrapping paper; markers; construction paper; tape.

To make the game: Read the poem below before making the game pieces. Copy the picture of Alexi in Figure F on a large sheet of wrapping

Figure F

paper, enlarging as much as possible. Copy drawings from Figure F in the item list (in a size proportional to the monster) on construction paper or drawing paper; cut out. Note that at least 2 items must be reproduced 9 times to accommodate the fourth and fifth verse of the poem as it stands. The 2 items that are made 9 times should be placed in a small box and the other, single items in another box. (For example, make 9 apples, 9 dogs, 1 lamp shade, 1 light bulb, 1 cup, 1 airplane, 1 cat, 1 baby buggy, 1 fork, and 1 hammer. Put the apples and dogs in one box and the rest in another box.)

To play the game: Children select pictures from 1 of the 2 boxes and sit neatly in a line. All of the pictures in the box containing the unrepeated items must be picked, and at least 1 each of the multiply drawn items must be picked. (Leftovers in the second box can be used by the adult storyteller to fill in the picture. This second box allows you to accommodate many more than 10 children at your story minute.) The children practice saying loudly what they are holding in their hand. After the children have rehearsed, the storyteller reads the poem, pausing at the blanks. At that moment, another adult taps the head of a child, signaling him or her to say what he or she is holding. The storyteller finishes the rest of the verse, pausing at the end so that the child can tape the picture onto the poster as indicated by the poem. The adult who is tapping the children needs to be familiar with the poem, and the point at which a child with a multiply drawn item must be tapped (verses 4 and 5). It really is funny, and the drawing is mighty odd by the end of the poem. When the game is completed, the storyteller should reread the poem without pause.

THIS IS ALEXI

She occasionally wears _____ (1)
  on her foot of blue
  instead of a shoe.

She always wears _____ (2)
  instead of a hat,
  now fancy that!

She puts a _____ (3)
  in her tummy
  which she thinks is yummy.

She wears _____ (4)
  up and down her 9 arms
  like a bracelet with charms.

Many hands she covers with _____ (5)
  in place of gloves or a mitten
  to keep her nails from being bitten.

On cold winter days she wears a _____ (6)
  instead of a warm coat.
  At least it's not a boat.

In summer she likes to swim and then
  she puts on a _____ (7) for a swimsuit
  and also a big brown boot.

Her head is covered with _____ (8)
  where there should be hair.
  Thank goodness she doesn't seem to care.
  (She even likes it bare!)

Hanging around her neck is a _____ (9)
  She sometimes adds to that a necklace,
  because her theory is more, not less.

Out of her mouth pops a _____ (10)
  sometimes when she talks,
  sometimes when she walks.

Her words are not far behind.
  She doesn't seem to mind.
  And, frankly, we like her kind.

Sample list of items: apple, dog, lamp shade, light bulb, cup, airplane, cat, baby buggy, fork, hammer.

Monsters on Parade (Monster Sticks)

Parades are always fun. The participants enjoy the attention, and the onlookers enjoy watching. Here the participants are truly worthy of attention as they carry crazy monsters on sticks.

Materials: Brightly colored poster board (1 sheet for 2 monsters); collage-type materials, such as pieces of sponge, fun fur, yarn, bells, pipe clean-ers, wadded tissue-paper balls, plastic eyes, circles made from fabric, paper spirals, etc.; a cardboard tube (roughly the size of the tube in a roll of gift wrap); glue; stapler; white Con-Tact paper; string; hole puncher.

To make a monster stick: Cut a crazy shape out of poster board. Heavily decorate the shape, keeping in mind that it is supposed to be a monster. Cover a wrapping paper tube with white Con-Tact paper to form the stick. Punch 2 holes near the bottom center of the monster shape,

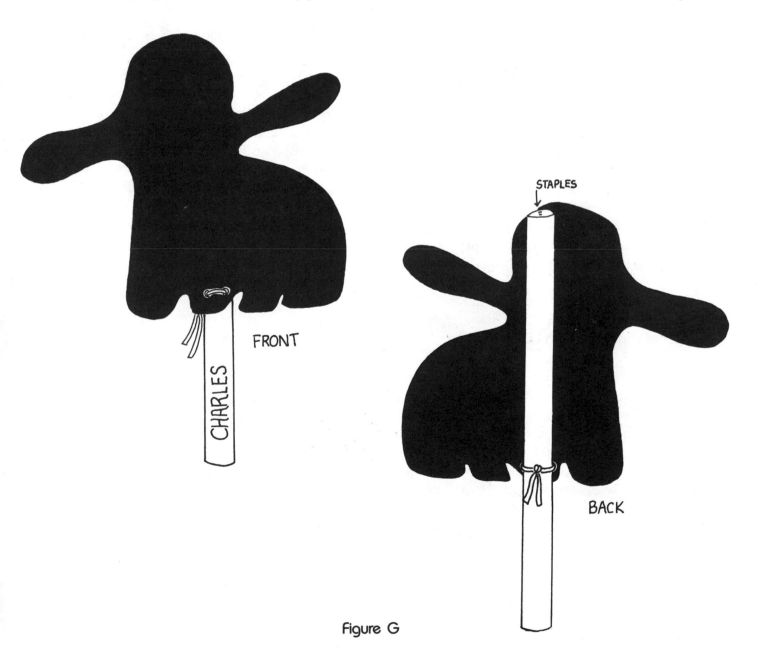

FRONT

CHARLES

STAPLES

BACK

Figure G

roughly 1½ inches apart. Center the holes against the stick and staple the top of the monster to the top front side of the stick. Tie a string through the holes and around the back of the stick. This construction is shown in Figure G. Label the stick with the child's name. Each child should have one to carry and take home.

 ## Make a Monster

Remarkably imaginative monsters can be made by children using balloons and a few other simple materials. Even more imagination will go into the naming of the monster.

Materials: Twelve-inch balloons; poster board (1 sheet for 8 monsters); various colors of Con-Tact paper; yarn or felt for the hair; wax paper; hole puncher.

To prepare for the monsters: Trace a feet pattern from Figure H; cut out. Trace around the edges of the pattern on cardboard; cut out. Use these feet as a template for the remaining monsters. Trace around the template on a piece of poster board; cut out. Punch a hole in the feet according to the placement shown in Figure H. To make the features, cut various eye, nose, ear, and mouth shapes from Con-Tact paper. Suggestions for features are shown in Figure I (see page 52). Simple wigs can be made by sticking ends of yarn or strips of felt along the edge of a circle of Con-Tact paper. For each ear, cut a front and back ear. Then stick these 2 together, except for the tab portion of the ears, which are left apart and bent at right angles (forward and backward) so that the ear can be stuck to a flat surface.

For each child: Attach feet to balloon and

have each child decorate it with stickers. Since peeling the backs off stickers may be too difficult for a child, prepare in advance a sheet of wax paper covered with the eyes, nose, mouth, ears, wig, freckles, and other shapes. When sticking the pieces to the wax paper, bend the corners of the sticker up slightly for easy removal. With the sticker-laden wax paper and a balloon with feet, the child can express monsterlike qualities in a quiet way.

Alternatives: This version of the balloon decoration uses assorted stickers that are sold in bags or boxes. Dots are readily available, as are various other shapes. These will simplify your task by reducing the number of hand-cut items on the menu. A commercial version of this game is also available, although it is not based on a monster theme. It is, nevertheless, modifiable. The package can be broken up so that several children can work from 1 box. Several packages may be required. A food art project, in which children decorate potatoes to look like monsters, is also an appropriate substitute.

Monster Cake

Top off a silly lunch of odd-shaped foods with this fabulous monster cake. This is an extremely easy-to-make and easy-to-decorate cake, since even the most lax interpretation will appear fun and monsterlike.

Materials: One 9 x 13-inch cake (see Cake Tips in "How to Use This Book"); 1 can or batch of white frosting; red or blue food coloring; round candies (Skittles); red shoestring licorice; rope licorice; miniature marshmallows; giant gum ball; 4 black jelly beans and 4 big marshmallows, or 4 jelly circles and 4 black jelly beans.

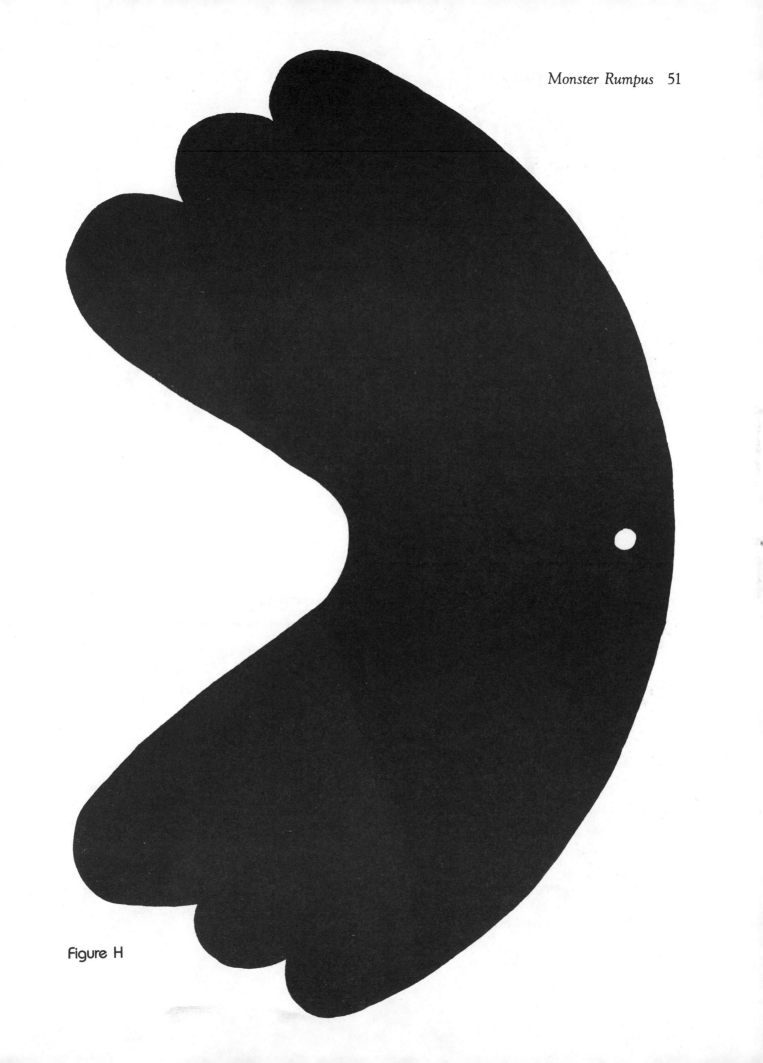

Figure H

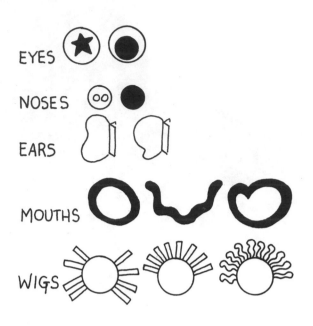

Figure I

To finish the cake: Following the pattern in Figure J, draw a full-size pattern for the cake on paper; cut out. Lay the pattern piece directly on the cake and cut along the edges with a sharp, large knife, keeping it as vertical as possible when cutting. Tint the frosting with red or blue food coloring. Ice the top and sides of the cake. Stick the eyes in place. Eyes can be either marshmallows with a black jelly bean poked into the center or jelly circles with a black jelly bean poked into the hole. Stick on a giant gum-ball nose and a rope licorice mouth. Stick Skittles and miniature marshmallows on the cake top, as shown in Figure K. Clip shoestring licorice to about 3–4 inches. Stick the licorice into the cake top as densely as you have the patience to do. The hairs should stand off the surface of the cake, roughly at a right angle. This cake is truly fun.

Suggestions

The interpretation of the monster theme presented here is quite tame and lovable. This guarantees that the theme is not provocative to any child in a negative way. Modifying the party theme to include more sting will make it more appealing to older children, but still we do not think it is worth the risk. It is charming and cranky enough to be monsterlike.

Accessorizing this party is simple. Spin-off products from some well-known television and fictional monster characters are available. Books featuring monsters, coloring books, crazy stickers without pictures, stickers with pictures, crazy glasses with eyes that pop off on coiled-wire attachments, pencils with monster tops, and so on are all available at novelty stores. Monster costume elements are also good favors.

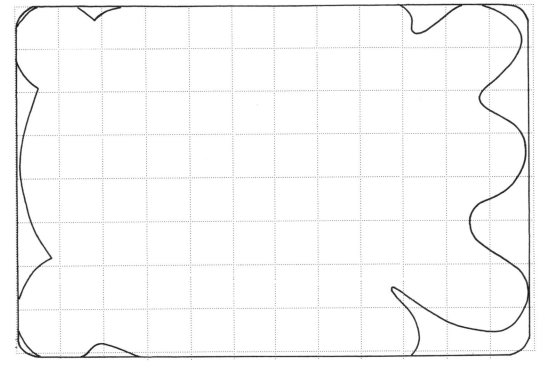

Figure J (1 sq. = 1 in.)

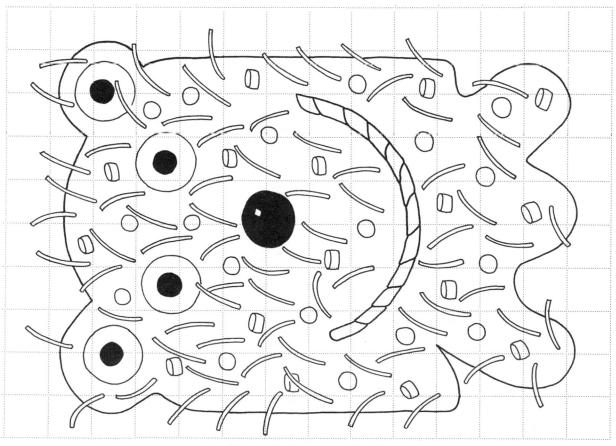

Figure K (1 sq. = 1 in.)

5

BABES IN PARTYLAND

AGE GROUP
4 to 5 years old

PARTY LENGTH
1½ hours

The Babes in Partyland theme is a natural for a young and spirited celebration. It capitalizes on children's innate love of rhythm and movement and the characters of their dreams—ballerinas and soldiers!

 The Plan

It all begins with the arrival of the Dancing Invitation—a "jointed" paper puppet "dressed" in tutu and ballet slippers or full military rega-

lia—which delivers the message and dances its way into the child's heart.

On the day of the party, play music to greet the children and set the mood as they arrive, readying them to dance and march along the Fanciful Footprint path. The footprints, by the way, are simple poster board cutouts laid out in a path to the gift drop-off and center of activities. Here, give the children their Beribboned Bands and Rat-a-Tat Hats, colorful poster-board creations that bring the ballerina and soldier theme alive. Direct the children to continue, following a maze of pink and blue streamers that go off in all directions but lead to the same destination—the

Sugarplum Fairy. Sweet are the faces that discover the goodies the fairy holds—easy-to-make Fantasy Bibs (snap-on costumes made of felt) or bags full of delicious morsels, ballerina stickers, and stick-on stars! With their booty in "toe," the children merrily march and dance a bit more, following the leader to the project table. At this time, the children sit and renew their energy while stringing colorful fabric "streamers" through a poster-board hoop. The result is a Fancy Hoop, a hand-held, colorful motion-object that will add a new element of fun to the children's dancing.

When they complete their hoops, turn up the music. Following a leader, the children may dance with their hoops, swinging them, tossing them, even putting them on their heads(!); they weave in and out of obstacles and finish off gathered in a circle, tossing up the hoops with a good loud cheer! Hooray! When the giggles subside and the children pick up their hoops, have them march over to the table to feast on a scrumptious and lovely Sugarplum Cake.

Music adds the finishing note to this party; now let the children supply it! Seat them in a circle and give each child an instrument—a kazoo, harmonica, pot or pan and spoon, toy drum, a string of bells, or whatever other noise-making objects you wish to use. The rest is up to them! Joining in with some favorite songs keeps the harmony flowing!

Dancing Invitations

These fanciful puppets dance right out of the envelope and into a child's heart, delivering the birthday message in style.

Materials: White poster board (1 piece for 16 invitations); pink and blue paper for the birthday message; colored fine-tip marking pens; small paper fasteners; hole puncher; ⅛-inch-wide ribbon (1 foot for each); envelopes. Optional decorations: string of sequins and tiny fabric flower for the ballerina; star sequins or stick-on stars, pipe cleaners, and silver or gold ⅛-inch-wide ribbon for the soldier; glue.

To make the pattern: Trace the ballerina and soldier parts on paper as shown in Figure A (ballerina) and Figure B (soldier); cut out. Trace the cutout patterns on cardboard, drawing along the outline; cut out. Use these cardboard pieces as the templates for making the ballerina and soldier.

For each invitation: Using the templates, trace the ballerina and soldier bodies and 2 legs for each on poster board; cut out.

To decorate the ballerina: Transfer the detail lines on the tracing paper onto the poster-board body and legs. Using colorful fine-tip markers, color in the hair, headband, eyes, nose, mouth, and belt on the ballerina body and the ballet slippers on the legs; outline the flower, leotard, and tutu. For an extra, decorative effect, glue a small piece of stringed sequins (or individual sequins) on the head for the headband and a fabric flower on the belt.

To decorate the soldier: Transfer the detail lines on the tracing paper onto the poster-board body and legs. Using colorful fine-tip markers, color the main part of the coat and the hat dark blue; the crossbands and narrow strip at the waistband red; the epaulets at the shoulder, the buttons, and sleeve braid yellow or orange; and the boots black. Color in the facial features as desired. For an extra, decorative effect, glue silver or gold ribbon along the crossbands and waistband, at the brim of the hat, and along the top edge of the boots; cut a very small piece of pipe cleaner and glue it on the center of the hat, top this and the crossbands off with a sequin or stick-on star—you'll have a 4-star general on your hands!

To complete both invitations: Carefully punch holes in the lower body and legs of the ballerina and soldier, using a hole puncher or very sharp scissors (see Figures A and B). Assem-

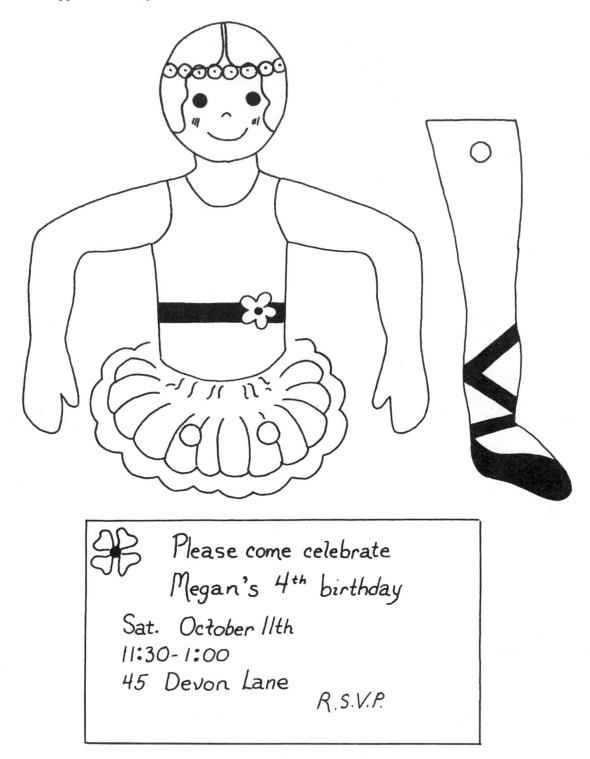

Please come celebrate
Megan's 4th birthday
Sat. October 11th
11:30-1:00
45 Devon Lane
R.S.V.P.

Figure A

Figure B

ble each by lining up the holes on the legs with those of the body; then, using paper fasteners stuck through the holes, secure the parts loosely together. Punch a hole at the top (head) of each and lace a 12-inch piece of ribbon through; tie a knot. Hold onto the ribbon and give the puppet a jiggle—it will dance before your eyes!

For the message, cut out a 2¼ x 4-inch piece of paper, write the details in, and slide the message between the body and the arms of the invitation.

Text: Put on your dancing (marching) shoes and join us to celebrate (child's name)'s birthday./ Date, Time, Place, R.S.V.P.

Alternatives: Ballet slippers and stars are commercially available in many forms, including stationery and all kinds of stickers. Use the decorative stationery or dress up plain postcards with stickers for an easy invitation. Or consider a ribbon-bordered postcard—simple and beautiful also! Just make a border of holes on a plain postcard, using a hole puncher, and weave pink and blue narrow ribbon through; secure with a bow and fill in the party message.

Beribboned Bands and Rat-a-Tat Hats

Beribboned bands and rat-a-tat hats are the kind of fanciful and fun props of which dreams are made.

Materials for the beribboned bands: Pink poster board (1 sheet for every 6 hats); ⅛-inch-wide purple ribbon (1 foot for each hat); ⅛-inch-wide white ribbon (2 feet for each hat); small fabric or felt flowers; glue; regular and double-stick tape; hole puncher; round-cord elastic; ruler.

To make the pattern: Trace the beribboned band section shown in the pattern section in the back of the book on paper; cut out. Transfer the cutout pattern onto cardboard, tracing along the outline; cut out. Using a ruler, measure and draw a 2 x 16-inch band pattern (rectangle) on cardboard; cut out. Use these cardboard pieces as the templates for the beribboned band.

For each hat: Trace the templates on poster board; cut out. Using a hole puncher, make a border of holes along the upper edge of the hat approximately ¼ inch apart, as shown in Figure C. In addition, punch 2 holes on the center of each flap about ¼ inch apart and ½ inch in from the bottom edge. Lace purple ribbon through the border holes and secure the ends on the back with tape. Lace white ribbon through each set of flap holes and tie in a bow (see Figure C). Glue

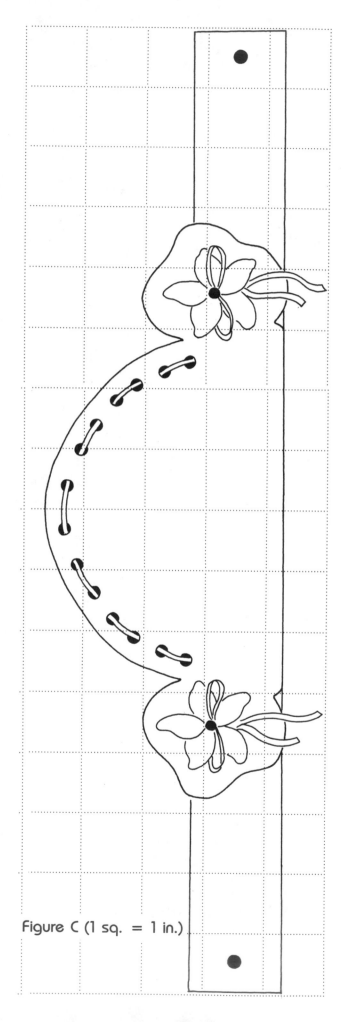

Figure C (1 sq. = 1 in.)

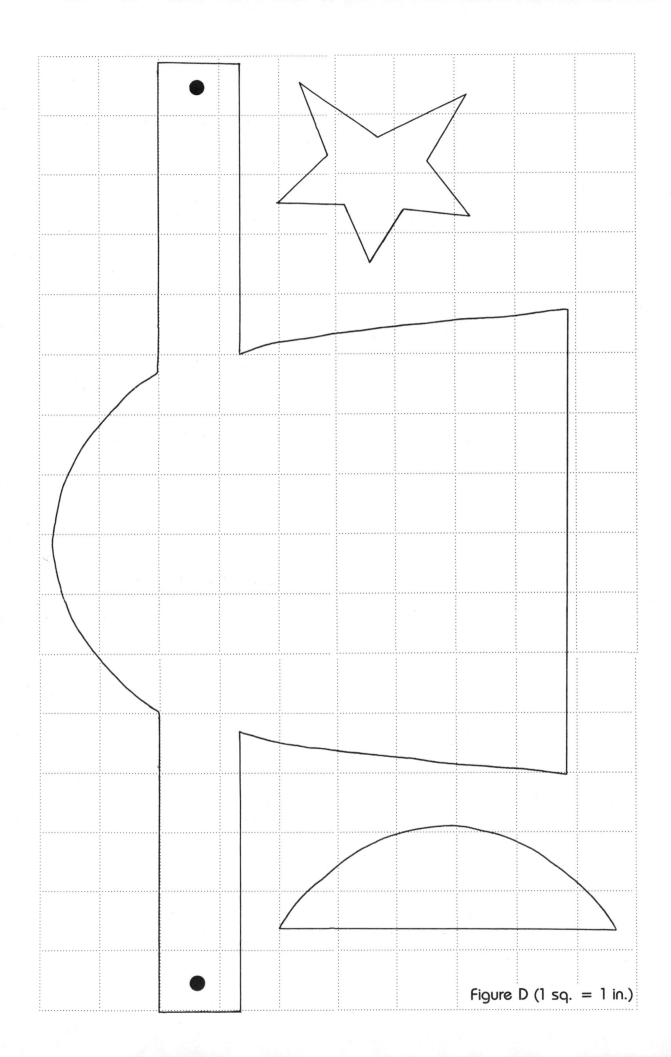

Figure D (1 sq. = 1 in.)

a fabric flower (either purchased or made as in the Ballerina Bibs section of this chapter) right above each white bow. Place double-stick tape or glue along back of the bottom, straight edge of the hat; do not tape or glue the flaps. Center the hat on the band, lining up the lower edges, and finger-press to secure the hat to the band (see Figure C). Punch holes at the end of the straight band and tie together with a 6-inch piece of round-cord elastic. Bend the flaps in slightly toward the hat, and you're finished!

Materials for the rat-a-tat hats: Blue poster board; red and yellow Con-Tact paper; red jumbo rickrack; large feathers; large star sequins (optional); glue; hole puncher; round-cord elastic.

To make the pattern: Draw the outline of the hat, brim, and star on paper, as shown in Figure D (see page 59); cut out. Transfer the cutout patterns onto cardboard, drawing along the outline; cut out. Use these cardboard pieces as the templates for making the hats.

For each hat: Trace the hat template on the blue poster board, the brim template on yellow Con-Tact paper, and the star on red Con-Tact paper; cut out. Affix the yellow Con-Tact paper to the brim of the poster-board hat, lining up the lower edges. Glue a 16-inch piece of rickrack along the entire headband, so that it is positioned slightly above the brim (see Figure E). Place the feather in the center of the hat. Affix the red Con-Tact paper star over the bottom of the feather to secure in place. Glue the sequin star to the red star (optional). Punch holes at the end of the straight band and tie together with round-cord elastic.

Alternatives: For the girls, you could make an easy and fun hair decoration out of fabric netting. Simply cut a 6-inch piece of netting the width of the fabric; accordion-fold the long edge and tie in the middle with a long piece of ribbon; then fan out the pleats. Use the dangling ends of the ribbon to tie the decoration in the hair! Or, easier

Figure E

yet, just tie a bunch of artificial or real flowers in each girl's hair. For the boys, cut out a 2 x 16-inch poster-board band and decorate it with stick-on stars and stripes. Punch holes at the ends of the band and tie together with round-cord elastic.

Fanciful Footprints

Fanciful footprints get the party goers in step as soon as they arrive. They can be used throughout the party when the children are dancing and marching. Just lay them down wherever you want the children to go!

Before the party, draw and cut out simple paper or poster-board footprints as shown in Figure F and lay them on the floor to form a path. You can use your own child's shoe to draw the footprint, by the way—simply trace around the bottom of the shoe on paper! At party time, instead of walking, have the ballerinas tiptoe and the soldiers march their way along the path.

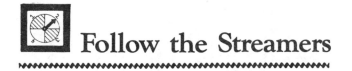

Figure F

Materials: Rolls of crepe-paper streamers; plastic bags full of goodies, ballet stickers, and stick-on stars; tape.

Before the party: Lay a variety of colorful streamers (1 color for each child or group of children) on the floor, going in all directions but ending at the same spot (an area that is large enough for all the children to gather together in). Tape the streamers to the floor every now and then to keep them in place.

At party time: You (or a helper) inconspicuously dress as the Sugarplum Fairy, with a beribboned band and a streamer necklace (several 5-foot lengths of streamers tied loosely around the neck), just before the streamer activity begins; then you get in position at the end of the streamers, surrounded with the goody bags and fantasy bibs (optional, discussed later in this chapter) that you are going to hand out. When ready to start, assign each child or group of children to a different streamer color. Give instructions to follow the streamer to its end, marching and dancing all the way! Don't be surprised if in the end, some of the streamers become part of a free-form dance!

Music Fest

Since music is such an integral part of this party, why not give the children a chance to make some music of their own? Gather them in a circle, sitting down, and pass out an instrument to each child—kazoos, pots, pans and spoons, harmonicas, strings laced with bells, drums, whatever noise-making things you wish to choose. To keep the harmony going, sing some of the children's favorite songs with them. They'll love it!

Follow the Streamers

A maze of pink and blue streamers takes over where the footprints leave off, keeping the party goers in step and on route to the Sugarplum Fairy!

 Fabulous-and-Festive Fancy Hoops

In the hands of the young, these simple hoops swirl and twirl and fly up high, creating waves of color and motion. A big hit with the children, fancy hoops are also extremely easy to make!

Materials: Pink and blue poster board (1 sheet for every 24 hoops); hole puncher; staples or glue; ruler; fabric scraps that are about 12 inches long or more, ribbons, rickrack, lace, yarn, felt strips (or whatever you can find to lace through small holes that is colorful and moves fluidly; use scraps or purchase remnants) in pastels for the ballerinas and primary colors for the soldiers; plastic bags.

To make each hoop: Using a ruler, measure and draw a rectangular strip that is 2 x 12 inches on poster board (pink for the ballerinas, blue for the soldiers); cut out. Use this as a template for tracing the rest of the hoops. Staple or glue the ends of the strip together to form a hoop. Using a hole puncher, punch holes in the middle of the hoop, spacing them about ½ inch apart along the circumference. Assemble the fabric scraps, rickrack, ribbons, etc., for decorating the hoops. Trim any pieces that need it; they should be narrow enough to fit through the holes. Divide the decorations evenly and place in a plastic bag for each child.

   At party time, give each child a hoop and a bag full of goodies. Start this colorful project with a short demonstration, showing them how to pull the pieces through the holes (see Figure G). When the hoops are complete (as shown in Figure H), the children will be ready for a gala performance of dancing and marching—twirling, shaking, flying, and tossing the hoops in the air as they go.

Alternatives: To add color and extra flair to the dancing without the fancy hoops, hand the children some scarves and streamers. Blowing bubbles and catching them is lots of fun, too!

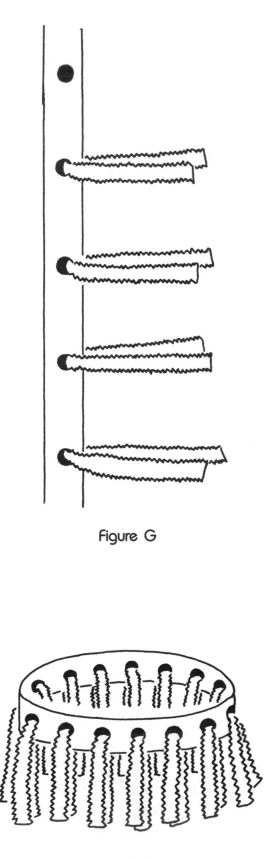

Figure G

Figure H

 **Fantasy Bibs**

Fantasy bibs are not the typical food-catching variety; they're great-looking, snap-on costumes, made almost entirely out of that wonderful, work-saving fabric—felt!

Materials for the ballerina bib: Pink and green felt (½ yard of 72-inch pink felt for every 6 bibs, ¼ yard of green for 6 bibs); fabric netting (1 yard for 6 bibs); square of purple felt for the flowers, plus bits of yellow felt for flower centers (optional); fusible webbing (available in fabric and notions stores) or glue; thread; snaps.

To make the ballerina bib pattern: Draw one 8½ x 13-inch rectangle (for the main body piece) and one 8½ x 1-inch rectangle (for the netting band) on a piece of paper; cut out. Draw a flower as in Figure I, making it about 1¾ inches in diameter; cut out. Trace the pink and green collar pieces shown in the pattern section at the back of the book on a large sheet of paper; cut out.

For each ballerina bib: Pin the large collar, the body, and the netting band patterns to pink felt, the smaller collar pattern to green felt, and the flower to purple felt (you'll need 3 flowers); cut all the pieces out. Using a pair of pinking shears or regular scissors, "scallop" the bottom edge of the body piece and both long edges of the netting band (see Figure J). Cut a 6-inch strip of netting the width of the fabric or at least 28 inches wide. To put the bib together, center the green felt collar slightly below the top edge of the body piece (see Figure J). Lightly glue, or fuse in place using fusible webbing according to manufacturer's directions. Lay the pink collar on top of the green, leaving approximately 1 inch of green felt exposed along the outer edges; glue or fuse in place (see Figure J). Glue 1 flower on each of the 3 center pink-collar scallops; glue a few tiny

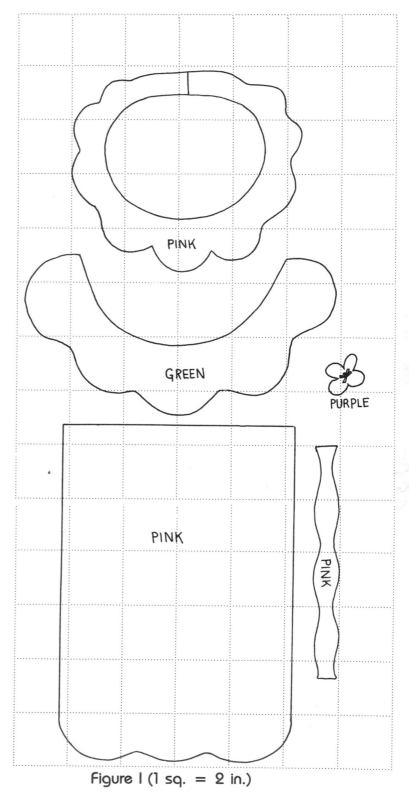

Figure I (1 sq. = 2 in.)

pieces of yellow felt on the center of each flower, if desired. Fold the netting in half lengthwise. Using a sewing machine or needle and thread, run a gathering (long) stitch along the folded edge

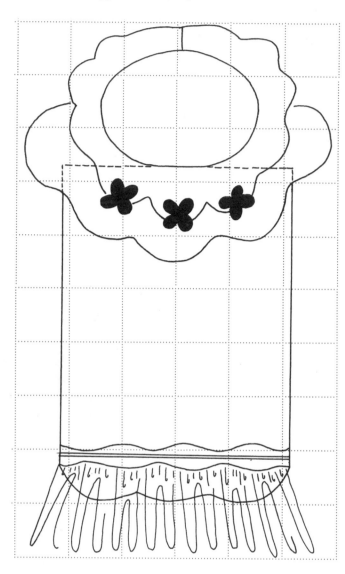

Figure J (1 sq. = 2 in.)

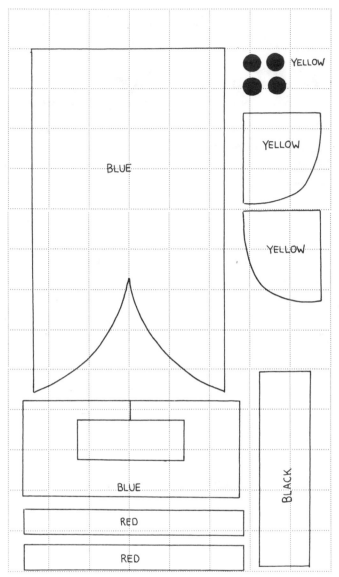

Figure K (1 sq. = 2 in.)

of the netting. Gather the netting to fit across the lower edge of the bib (8½ inches); stitch in place. Place the pink felt netting band over the top edge of the gathered netting to conceal the netting edge; stitch the band in place (see Figure J). Sew a snap on the back, and the bib is ready for dancing!

Materials for the soldier bib: Blue, red, yellow, and black felt (½ yard of 72-inch blue felt, ¼ yard each of red and yellow, and ⅛ yard of black for every 6 bibs); glue or fusible webbing; snaps.

To make the soldier bib pattern: Draw the scaled outline of the bib pieces as shown in Figure K on a large piece of paper; cut out.

For each soldier bib: Pin the body and collar piece on blue felt, the crossbands on red felt, the epaulets (shoulder pieces) and buttons on yellow felt, and the waistband on black felt; cut out all the pieces, using pinking shears or regular scissors. To put the bib together, lay the red crossbands on the body piece, so that they cross in the center and start at the top corners; glue, or fuse in place using fusible webbing and following manufactur-

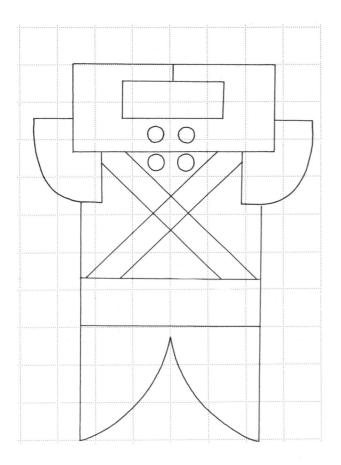

Figure L (1 sq. = 2 in.)

out each bib in 1 piece. Color in the details with marking pens. For the tutu, instead of netting, gather up a length of crepe-paper streamer and glue or tape it in place, if desired.

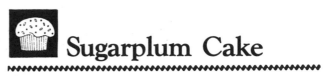

Sugarplum Cake

You can easily transform a simple Bundt cake into a floral delight with store-bought decorations, gel, and frosting.

Materials: One Bundt cake; 1 can or 1 recipe of white frosting; 1 tube of decorating gel; 2 to 3 packages floral cake decorations (available in the cake-decorating section of grocery stores); pink food coloring.

To finish the cake: Tint the frosting pink and cover the entire cake with frosting. Using the natural curves in the Bundt cake as a guide, pipe lines of decorating gel; alternate, starting from the center opening and going almost to the bottom, outer edge of the cake and then to about 2½ inches from the bottom edge. Place a floral decoration at the end of each line or just at the edge of the longest lines. Pipe a decorative circle along the bottom edge of the cake (see Figure M, page 66). Add a few candles, and the cake is ready to be devoured.

er's directions. Next, lay the epaulets on the top corners of the body piece, overlapping the pieces about 1 inch along the sides (see Figure L); glue or fuse in place. Center the collar at the top of the main body piece so that it overlaps the epaulets and crossbands by approximately 1 inch; glue or fuse in place. Center 2 buttons on the collar and 2 about ¾ inch lower on the body piece; glue or fuse in place. Lay the waistband on the body piece, so that it covers the ends of the crossbands (see Figure L); glue or fuse in place. To finish off the bib, fringe the epaulets, making 1-inch slashes perpendicular to the outer edge. Sew a snap on the back collar, and the bib is ready for service!

Alternative: Make similar ballerina and soldier bibs by drawing the outline of the assembled bibs (as in Figures J and L) on poster board and cutting

Suggestions

There are many commercially available products with ballerina and soldier motifs that coordinate with this party—ballet stickers, stationery, stamp pads, barrettes and other hair fasteners, headbands, leg warmers, necklaces, charms, etc.; soldier figures and paraphernalia, medals, star and stripe stickers, stationery, stamp pads, coloring books, storybooks, etc. Keep these in mind when buying treats, prizes, or favors and when looking for substitutions for party elements described in this chapter.

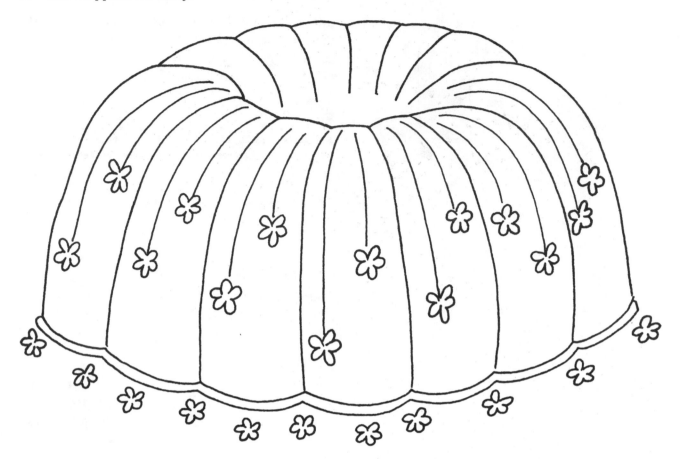

Figure M

DINOSAUR DIGS

┌─────────────────────────────┐
│   │
│   AGE GROUP   │
│   4 to 6 years old   │
│   │
│   PARTY LENGTH   │
│   1½ to 2 hours   │
│   │
└─────────────────────────────┘

Dinosaurs may have left this world millions of years ago, but they live on in the dreams and fantasies of the young. Children and dinosaurs are a classic combination. Something about the mix of fascination and intrepidation is very appealing. And the Latin names add to the mystery and fun! Here's a party that capitalizes on dinosaur mania. We've found it seduces even children who haven't discovered what all the hubbub is about!

 **The Plan**

The fun begins with the invitation—a simple dinosaur shape that the children decorate at home, sign, and bring along to the party for a Dino Art Show. You can draw it as illustrated in the instructions, trace it from a book, or glue a dinosaur picture on paper and cut it out (the children can decorate the back). You'll be amazed at the enthusiasm this invitation generates. It provides both a creative and learning experience and sets the mood for more!

As the children arrive at the party, send them along a path of Dinosaur Prints—simple paper cutouts—to an area where they hang their artwork and relinquish their gifts. Then have the children go off on a "Dig" to look for hidden bones (again, cut from paper) or for plastic dinosaurs or eggs. Once some of youth's energy is expended, gather them together to sit and view the clothesline Dino Art Show. With much pomp, a "judge" can examine the artwork, declare each dino a winner—the funniest, ugliest, most colorful, etc.—and present each artist with a Dinosaur Medallion of Honor, plus a well-deserved round of applause! Hand out the hats—in this case, replicas of a dinosaur head—and send the children stomping off dinosaur-style to the traditional birthday feast. Now the fantasy really comes alive. Along with the birthday song come howls and growls and the eating of a Dastardly Dinosaur Cake!

The grand finale can be a project or game, both are amusing and entertaining. For the project, the children make Edible Dinos from marshmallows, pretzels, raisins, etc. They're kooky and delicious and as creative as can be, and they provide a sweet take-home favor, too! As for games, have the children create Dinosaur Shadows with their hats on, dramatizing the dinosaurs as they roamed the wilds! (You'll be amazed at how effective the shadows are!) Then, for a calming effect, it's nice to finish off with a round of "Who Am I? What Am I?" using dinosaur names and related words—bones, fossils, museum, etc. When the doorbell rings announcing the end of the celebration, send the children off with beaming faces topped by dinosaur hats, medallions, perhaps an edible creature, some paper bones, and—if that isn't enough—with a Surprise Dino Egg made of crepe paper rolled up around some goodies! There's no doubt the dinosaur will live on in their minds, along with wonderful party memories!

Color Me a Stegosaurus

"Color Me a Stegosaurus" gets the party rolling before anyone rings the doorbell. Each child receives a paper stegosaurus with party details and a request to decorate the dino and bring it to the party for a dino art show!

Materials: Light-colored construction paper or art paper; fine-tip marking pen; large envelopes.

To make the pattern: Draw the outline of the dinosaur as shown in Figure A on a large piece of paper; cut out. Transfer the cutout pattern onto cardboard, drawing along the outline; cut out. Use this cardboard piece as the template for making the invitations.

For each invitation: Trace the template on light-colored construction or art paper; cut out. Leave one side of the invitation blank (for the artwork). On the other side, using a fine-tip marking pen, draw in the eye and mouth as shown in Figure A. Then fill in the birthday text. Be sure to include the guest's name on the invitation for easy identification of the dinos at the party. Slip the dino into the envelope and on its way and watch those dinos come back to life!

Text: I'm not yet prehistoric—I'm going to be 5! Please come celebrate with me, (child's name)./ Name, Date, Time, Place, R.S.V.P./Nobody knows exactly what dinosaurs looked like. Please color, paint, or decorate me the way you think I looked and BRING ME TO THE PARTY./P.S. We'll have a DINO ART SHOW!

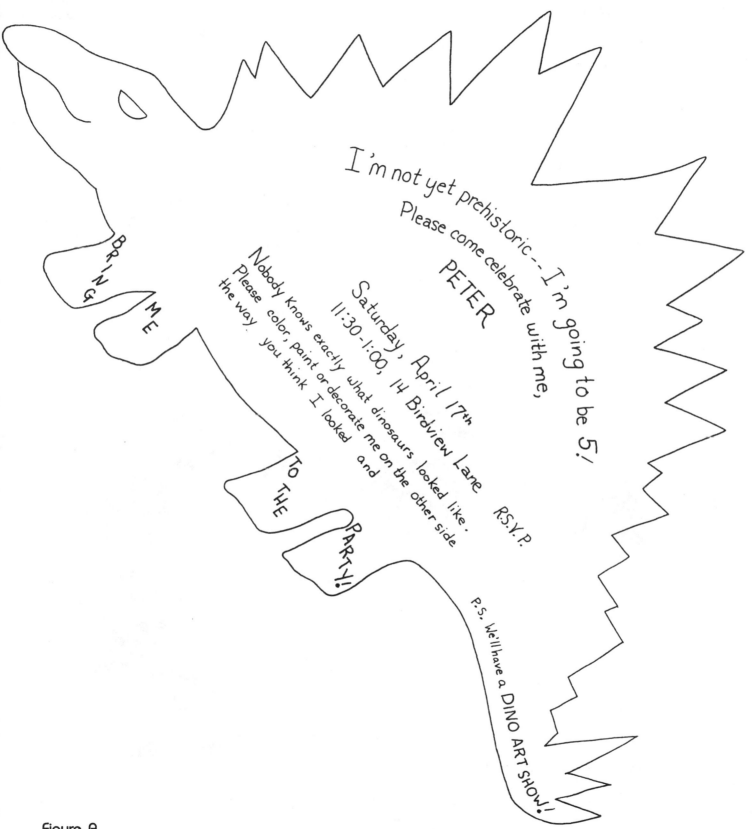

I'm not yet prehistoric -- I'm going to be 5!

Please come celebrate with me,

PETER

Saturday, April 17th
11:30-1:00, 14 Birdview Lane   R.S.V.P.

Nobody knows exactly what dinosaurs looked like.
Please color, paint or decorate me on the other side
the way you think I looked and

BRING

ME

TO THE

PARTY!!

P.S. We'll have a DINO ART SHOW!

Figure A

Dino Heads

Dino heads put the children in the dinosaurs' shoes . . . or should we say heads!

Materials: Green poster board (1 piece for every 2 hats); red and blue Con-Tact paper; 2 large wiggle eyes; ruler; double-stick tape; glue; black marking pen; round-cord elastic; hole puncher.

To make the pattern: Trace the dinosaur head, eye, horns, and scales shown in the pattern section at the back of the book on a large sheet of paper (this head is also shown here, reduced, as Figure B); cut out. Transfer the cutout patterns onto cardboard, drawing along the outlines; cut out. Using a ruler, draw a rectangular band 1 x 16 inches on cardboard; cut out. Use these cardboard pieces as the templates for making the hats.

For each hat: Trace the head template twice on green poster board for a left face and a right face and the band once; cut out. Trace the eye and scale templates on red Con-Tact paper and the horn templates on blue Con-Tact paper for each side of the face; cut out. Working on one side of the face at a time, affix the Con-Tact paper horns, scales, and eye piece to the poster-board

Figure B (1 sq. = 1 in.)

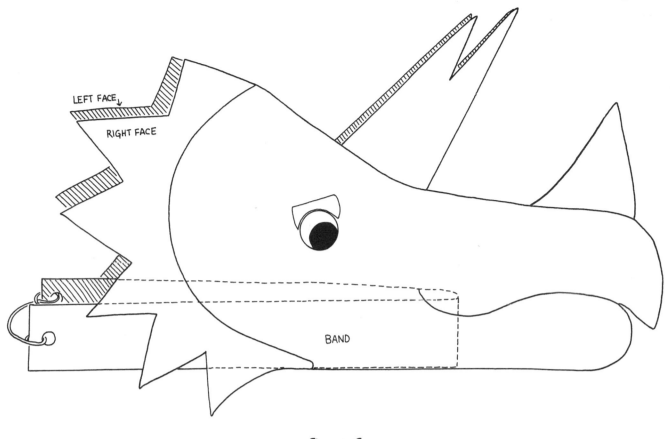
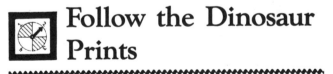
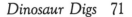

Figure C

face; glue the wiggle eye on to the eye piece, as shown in Figure B. Using the marking pen, draw in the mouth on both faces as shown. On the wrong side of 1 face piece, apply small pieces of double-stick tape along the top edge, horns, snout, and chin (the tape should not extend beyond the face edges). Place the 2 face pieces together, right sides out and edges aligned; finger-press to secure together. Fold the band in half and place between the attached face pieces, along the lower edge and about halfway in, as shown in Figure C. Using double-stick tape, secure the band in place. Punch holes at the ends of the straight band and tie together with a 6-inch piece of round-cord elastic.

Try it on and see if you don't feel a little bit like a dinosaur!

Follow the Dinosaur Prints

Create a path for the children to follow out of simple, large paper footprints, leading them to the "clothesline" (where they can hang up their decorated dinos) and to the gift depot. Cut the prints freehand or trace the one in Figure D on cardboard to make a template. Trace around the template on construction or art paper and cut out. Be sure to cut plenty (you can cut through more than 1 layer of paper at a time to get multiple prints from 1 cut!). The minute the first guest arrives, start him or her along the path. It brings the dinosaur out in everybody!

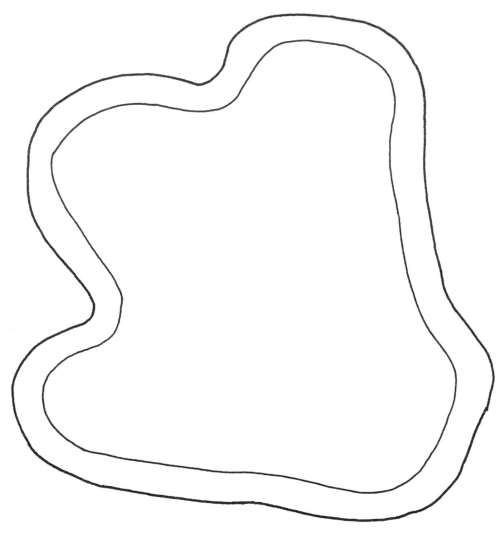

Figure D

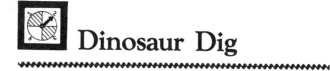

Dinosaur Dig

If it weren't for "digs," we wouldn't know about dinos! For this simple search, cut out lots (100+) of simple bone shapes from light-colored scrap paper as shown in Figure E. Don't hesitate to cut them out freehand—bones don't look perfect, especially when they've been underground for millions of years! If desired, outline the bone shape with a green marking pen or crayon.

On the day of the party, hide the bones around the party area; then at party time, send the children in all directions—with bags in hands—in search of dinosaur bones. Have extra bones to hide to make sure that no one ends up without any bones!

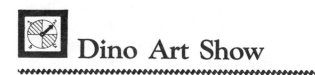

Dino Art Show

What fun it is to see how each child decorates his dino. String them up for all to admire!

Before the party, string up a line with clothespins, at child's eye level, for hanging up the dinos. If possible, the line should be placed in an area

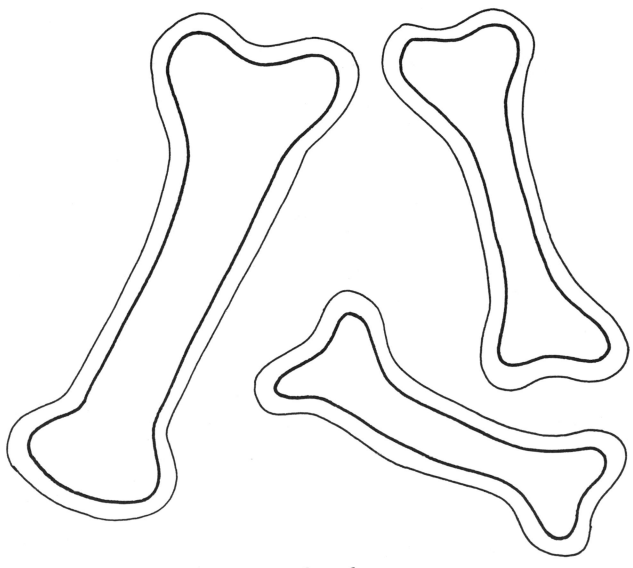

Figure E

where there is enough room for the children to sit around and "gaze" at the art!

At party time, assemble the children in a circle near the art show and, with much pomp, begin the judging ceremonies. The judge (Mom, Dad, or a helper) examines each piece and then declares each dino a winner for a different reason, e.g., the funniest, most colorful, scariest, ugliest, prettiest, etc. Each child is given his or her own moment to shine; place a Dinosaur Medallion (see page 74) around his or her neck and encourage all to join in with a round of applause. Watch the little faces beam with delight and pride.

Dinosaur Shadow Play

Not many youngsters have a large repertoire of shadow puppets, but that doesn't matter—this shadow-play game is strictly rated, "No experience necessary." All you have to do is shine some lights on the party goers, decked out in their dino head hats. Instruct them to create some hand motions, and the "beasts" will come alive! It's simple, but terrific!

Dinosaur Medallion of Honor

Here's a medal that will be cherished long after the party is over. For extra-long life, make it from felt; otherwise, poster board will do just fine.

Materials: Green felt (2 squares for 4 medallions); glue or fusible webbing (available in fabric stores); thread or black marking pen; stick-on circles for the eyes (optional; available at stationery and craft stores); yarn; hole puncher.

To make the pattern: Trace the outline of the dinosaur in Figure F on paper; cut out.

To make each medallion: First put 2 squares of felt together to form a single layer. To do this, either fuse the 2 pieces together, using fusible webbing and following manufacturer's directions, or glue the pieces together and let dry. You'll now have 1 extra-thick square of felt. Pin the pattern to the felt; cut out. If desired, you can make a stitching line from the back of the head to the tail to define the scales, as in Figure F, and also at the mouth (not shown in Figure F). Or you can draw in the line and mouth with a fine marking pen.

Using a hole puncher, punch 2 holes along the top of the dino. Thread a 30-inch piece of yarn through and tie to secure. Stick a circle eye on each side of the dino's head, if desired, and you

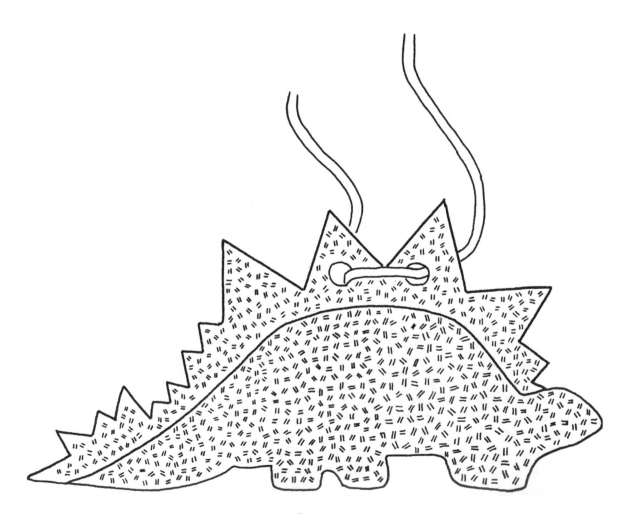

Figure F

have a medallion that any dino lover would be proud to wear!

Alternative: For a poster-board dino, simply trace the pattern on poster board; cut out. Draw in the details with a marking pen and finish off as for the felt medallion.

Edible Dinos

Half the fun of this project is in the eating! With very little fuss on your part, you can involve the children in a creative project that will bring on the giggles and will taste delicious, too!

Before the party, assemble marshmallows, thin pretzel sticks, spice drops, raisins, cheese snacks, and any other soft edibles and place in a paper bowl or cup for each child. Along with these include some plastic mixer straws (short, narrow ones).

At the party, each child creates a dinosaur by sticking marshmallows together with straws and embellishing the "body" with goodies attached to straws and pretzel sticks (see Figure G). You can stick some of the candies on the straws before the party or let the children do it all themselves. Either way, it's a barrel of laughs!

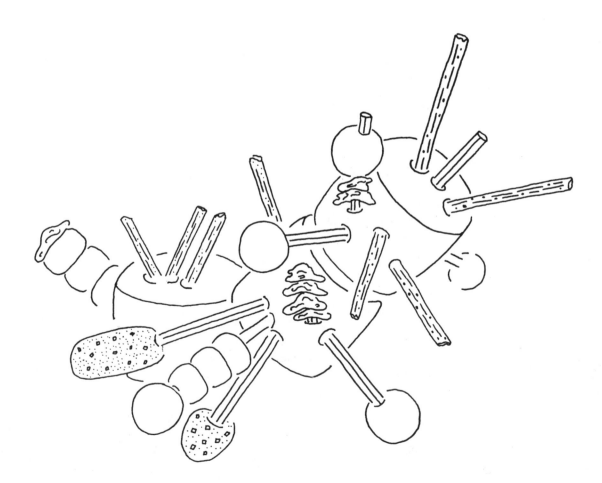

Figure G

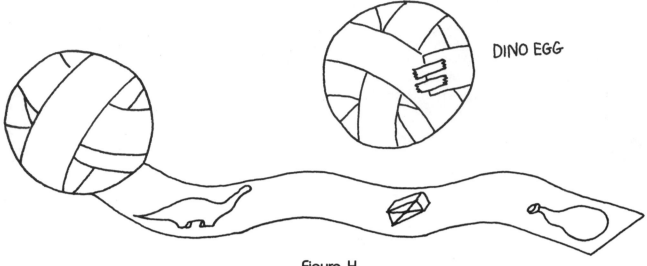

DINO EGG

Figure H

Surprise Dino Eggs

A bit of dinosaur memorabilia walking out with each guest will keep the dino spirit alive. To make surprise eggs, simply roll up a store-bought plastic dino and some candies or other dinosaur souvenirs—e.g., stickers, erasers, sponges, stamps, etc.—one at a time, in green crepe-paper streamer to form an egg shape. Tape the end to secure and add a dino sticker if desired. At home, as the child unrolls the egg, the goodies fall out (see Figure H).

Dastardly Dinosaur Cake

Deliciously beastly and guaranteed to create laughs galore, this creation starts with a 9 x 13-inch cake made from a mix. It looks so wonderful that even the dino hats want to delve in!

Materials: One 9 x 13-inch cake (see Cake Tips in "How to Use This Book"); 2 cans or 1½ batches white frosting; green food coloring; candies—candy corn, watermelon slices, jelly circles, or candies of your choice.

To finish the cake: Following the pattern shown in Figure I, draw a full-size pattern on paper for all the pieces and cut out (the shaded areas are not part of the pattern, they're extra). Lay the pattern pieces directly on the cake and cut along the edges with a sharp, large knife, keeping it as vertical as possible when cutting. Place the body piece on a very large platter (at least 20 inches) or on a large piece of heavy cardboard covered with aluminum foil. Assemble the cake, as shown in Figure J, affixing the mouth to the body first, then the horn to the upper mouth piece, the tail to the end of the body, and all 4 legs. Use some of the frosting, tinted green, to "glue" the pieces together. Frost the entire cake with the green frosting. To form the scaly skin, dip the end of a spoon in hot water and press it into the frosting, making a "dip" pattern. You can do this in rows or do it randomly, just try to cover the entire cake (it takes almost no time at all, and the effect is terrific). To complete, add the watermelon slices along the scales, end, and horn; the candy corn along the curve of the back and on the legs; and the jelly circle for the eye. To form the teeth, stick 2 rows of candy corn into the upper and lower mouth openings, as shown in Figure J, page 78.

While cutting the cake at the party, have the children make dinosaur sounds and name some of the different dinosaurs they know—it will tide them over until the cake enters their mouths!

Alternatives: Some easier cake options are (1) using dinosaur cookie cutters, press the dinosaur shapes into the frosting on a sheet cake and fill in the outlines with sprinkles; (2) using decorating gel, trace around the dino-head hat pattern, footprints, and bones on top of a cake; (3) simply place a lineup of plastic dinosaurs and perhaps some plastic trees on the cake; (4) have your local bakery make a cake with a dino design on top!

Suggestions

A tremendous number of commercially available products coordinate with this party—figures, stickers, stationery, coloring books, and information books, etc. Keep these in mind when buying treats, prizes, or favors and when looking for substitutions for party elements described in this chapter.

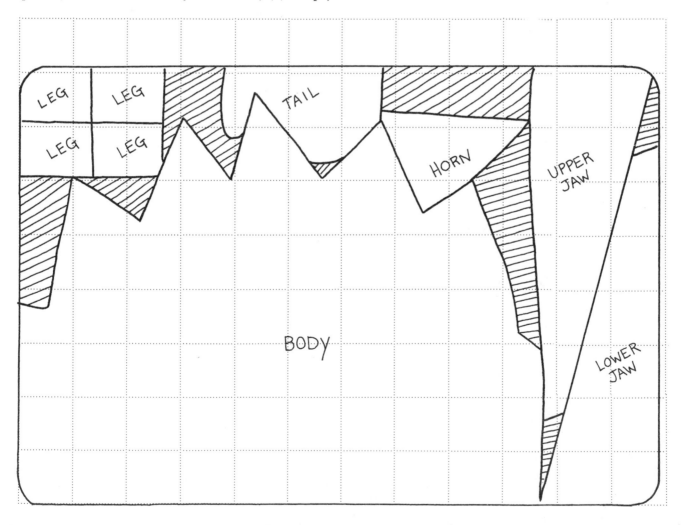

Figure I (1 sq. = 1 in.)

Figure J

7

BY THE SEA

Here is a fresh party theme for all those nurturing a year-round love affair with sea life. The wild assortment of life forms enlisted in playing out the party theme recreates an underwater fantasia for simple, clean fun.

 The Plan

The invitation—the Sea-View Funglasses—will initiate the children into an aquatic world. Looking through them, children can well imagine themselves deep in the sea. This play activity will

be a fun reminder of the party day to come. Begin the party itself with a clapping, snapping pair of Scallops. Use these mitts and balloons for many informal games that may last until well after all the children have arrived. Then have children disperse in a mad search for hidden seashells (or other theme treats). Next, direct Crab Walk races across a room or yard, where the purpose is simply to cross the field, and end the games with a silly crab parade to the eating area.

The smell and sight of good things to eat will transform the crabs . . . into fish! Wearing the exciting Fish Motion Hats, children will glide through the luncheon and cake servings with enthusiasm. Having the children do Fish Imitations, an hysterical exercise of imagination, will fill the time as you set or clear the table. The Whale Cake will reinforce the cheerful, bright feeling that water life inspires.

After refreshments, have the children elaborate on their view of sea life in an art project. Making simple Seascapes with precut fish, octopi, whales, snails, sea horses, coral, rocks, seaweed (bits of evergreen), and bubbles (sequins and glitter), which are then covered in pink or blue cellophane, will entertain the children and give them a very special memento of the day. Deep Sea Fishing is the natural follow-up to this project. In this uncommonly gratifying game, children search for rewards using a stick pole and "hook." The catch can be strung up on the string Tom Sawyer–fashion or put in a party bag to be taken home.

Next, change the picture by introducing simple, lightweight Blow Boats for racing. On a polished, smooth table or floor, these boats sail along powered by kid-wind.

This party can be either an indoor or an outdoor party. When scheduling an outdoor party, take the weather into account (sun, heat, rain). Including water play creates the need for greater adult supervision and careful scheduling. Wet or dry, indoors or outdoors, summer or winter, this party will be a novelty.

Sea-View Funglasses

Stylish, inventive eye wear announces the birthday of your youngster—an invitation to wear. Put them on and imagine what the world would look like if you lived in water!

Materials: Bright-colored poster board (1 sheet for 16 invitations); blue- or green-colored cellophane; glue; round-cord elastic; hole puncher; envelopes.

To make pattern: Trace the outline and inner line of the funglasses on paper following Figure A; cut along both lines. Transfer the cutout pattern onto cardboard. Use this cardboard piece as a template for the glasses.

For each invitation: Trace funglasses frame template on poster board; cut out. Cut a square of cellophane slightly larger than the entire frame (roughly 5 x 8 inches). Apply a thin layer of glue to the back side of the funglasses frame. Lay the frame, glued side down, on the square of cellophane and weight it down with a book or other heavy object until the glue dries. Afterward, trim the cellophane along the outside edge of the frame. Punch holes at the sides of the frame, as indicated in Figure A. Write the invitation message on the front of the frame or on a separate card enclosed in the envelope. Adjust the text to suit the particulars of your party (indoor/outdoor, lunch/afternoon, water play/dry, clothing, sun block, time, date (raindate?), place, etc.) and give instructions on how properly to use the glasses for fun and games. Tie a 20-inch piece of round-cord elastic through the holes to form a band that will hold the frames on the sea, sand, and sun lovers. Adjust these bands, using your child's head for sizing before sending.

Text: Wear these glasses and imagine you are a fish . . ./Swim on over to (child's name)'s and celebrate a birthday!/Date, Time, Conditions, Place, RSVP.

Alternatives: A simple whale (pictured in Figure G) cut out of poster board with party information written on the back; photographs of tropical fish, coral, etc., cut out of a nature magazine and pasted on a piece of white cardboard with party information on the back; shell stationery or cards, with party information on the inside, front, or back, all make desirable invitations for this party.

Figure A

Fish Hat

A fish-eyed, floppy-fin hat will get even the most reluctant guest into the mood of the party. The hat becomes less abstract when the fin begins to move, and then eyes begin to bulge!

Materials: White, black, and clear Con-Tact papers; colored poster board (1 sheet for 4 hats); round-cord elastic; ruler; hole puncher.

To make the pattern: Trace the outlines of the band, eye white, eye black, an entire fin piece (with spines), and a fin piece showing only the prongs, from the pattern section at the back of the book, on a large sheet of paper. Using a ruler, extend the lines marked by the arrows: extend the band equally on each side of the eyes to a total finished length of 18 inches; extend the fin piece showing only the prongs so that the straight segment measures 14 inches. Draw a rectangle 3½ x 1½ inches for the stiffener pattern. Cut out the paper patterns. Transfer the cutout patterns onto cardboard, drawing along the outline of the pattern piece; cut out. Use these cardboard pieces as templates for the hats.

82

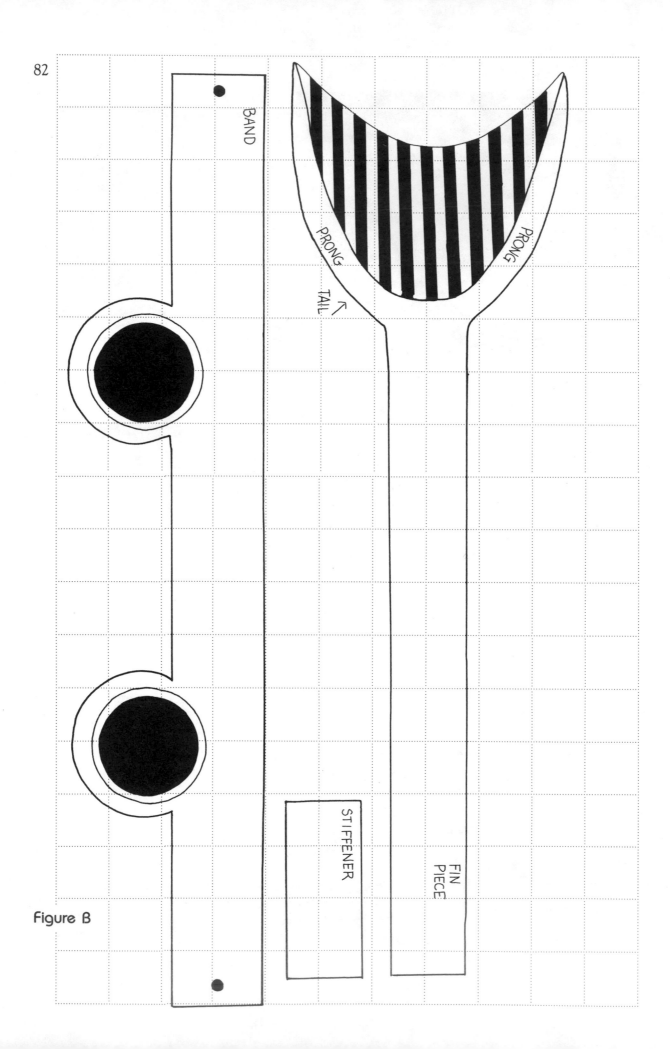

BAND

PRONG

TAIL

PRONG

STIFFENER

FIN PIECE

Figure B

For each hat: Trace the band, stiffener, and prong fin piece templates on poster board; cut out. Trace the eye whites and centers on white and black Con-Tact paper; cut out. Apply the black center to the eye white, and the entire eye to the headband, as shown in Figure B. Cut narrow (roughly ⅛ inch) strips of poster board 4 inches long to make spines in the fin piece. Cut two 6-inch squares of clear Con-Tact paper. Stick 1 in place on the underside of the hat, so that when you turn the hat over the sticky side faces up (showing through the area between the prongs on the fin piece). Placement of the clear Con-Tact paper is indicated in Figure C by a dotted line. Lay strips of poster board in place to form the spines, trimming the top to the curve of the prong (they will adhere to the Con-Tact paper); top with the second square of clear Con-Tact paper. Trim the spines to the final shape of the whole fin piece template, as shown in Figure B. Trim the excess Con-Tact paper along the outside edges of the prongs. To construct the hat, lay the headband

finished-eyes side down; using double-stick tape, attach the straight end of the fin piece flush with the bottom edge of the band. Affix the stiffener with double-stick tape, flush with the bottom edge. Try the hat on, holding the ends of the band together. The fin piece should float over the head (see Figure D).

Occasionally, when the poster board is particularly limp, the fin piece loses its lift and rests on the head. If this is the case, add another stiffener in the same place. Punch holes near the ends of the headband and tie with round-cord elastic. Store the hat flat until the party.

Figure D

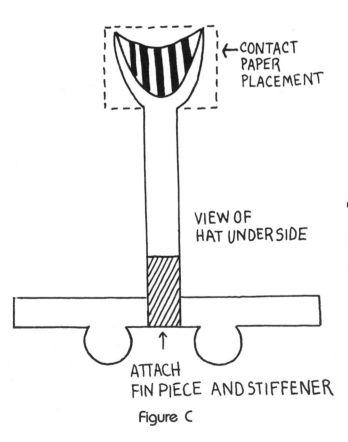

←CONTACT PAPER PLACEMENT

VIEW OF HAT UNDERSIDE

ATTACH FIN PIECE AND STIFFENER

Figure C

Scallop Squeeze Mitts

Slip on a scallop mitt, add balloons, and see the variety of silly games that ensue. Snap the scallop closed to catch a balloon and squeeze it again to send the balloon flying in the air. The mitt adds excitement to the simplest games of balloon volleyball, balloon catch, and keep the balloons aloft.

Materials: Pastel-colored poster board (1 sheet for 12 mitts); felt; glue; round-cord or narrow, flat elastic; balloons.

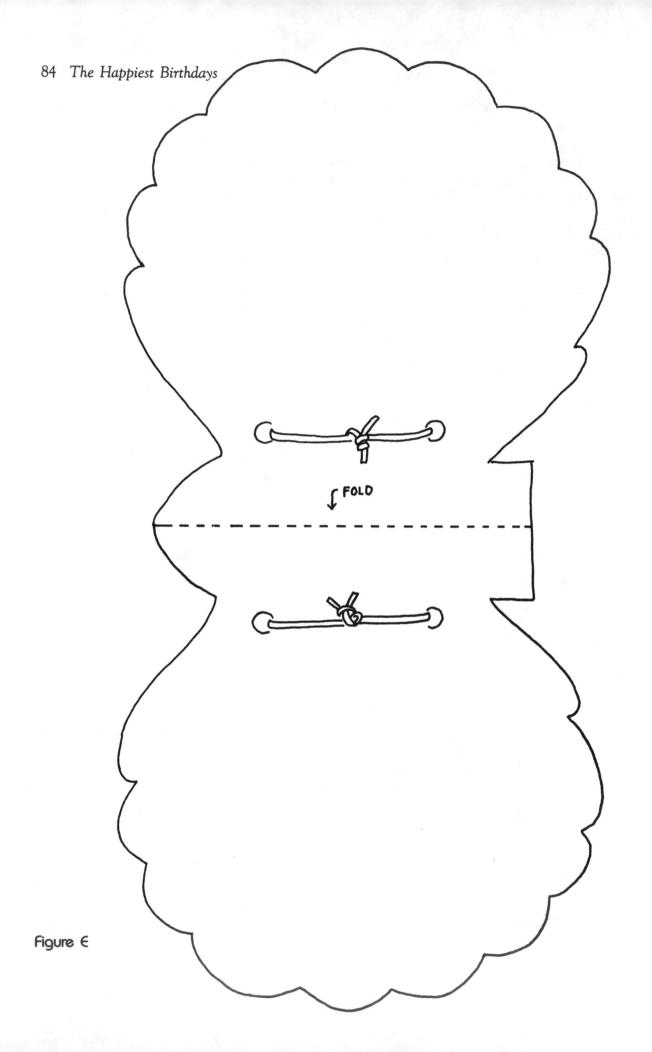

FOLD

Figure E

To make the pattern: Trace the scallop in Figure E on paper; cut out. Transfer the cutout pattern onto cardboard, drawing along the outline; cut out. Use this piece as a template for mitts.

For each mitt: Trace around the scallop mitt template on poster board; cut out. Cut a piece of felt larger than the scallop (approximately 7 x 11 inches). Glue the poster-board scallop to the surface of the felt. (Put the glue on the dull side of the poster board, if there is a dull side.) After the glue dries, trim the felt to the edges of the poster-board scallop. Fold the scallop in half along the fold line and punch 4 holes, as indicated in Figure E. Using two 5-inch pieces of elastic, tie a loop of elastic on each half shell, knotting the elastic on the inside (poster-board side).

To operate the mitt: Slip a thumb through the bottom elastic loop and a few fingers through the top loop; see Figure F. Snap the scallop closed and open. Test the mitt on different sizes of balloons (try a 10- or 12-inch balloon blown up to 6 inches), to see which size works best with the finished mitt. It should be possible to squeeze the mitt closed to send the balloon flying. Have at least 1 balloon of that size on hand for each child.

 # Shell Hunt

Hide shells in the sandbox, yard, or house, or on the beach if your beach lacks them for children to find. If you don't live near a traditional source of shells, buy something inexpensive that is decorated with shells and pick or cut them off. Craft stores and museums often sell shells in bags.

 # Crab Walk

A traditional children's racing game—the crab walk—is ideally suited to this party. To be a crab, you sit down, put your hands behind you on the floor, and bend your knees with feet planted in front of them. Then you do the impossible by raising your bottom in the air so that your body forms a flat table. Now walk!

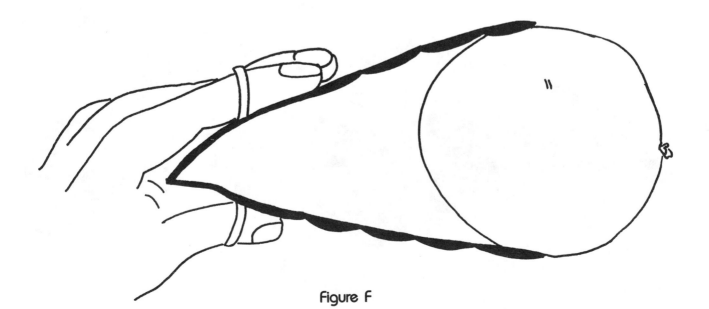

Figure F

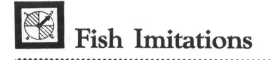

Fish Imitations

Pretending to be a fish is no easy task. Telling children to put on their best fish face and make real fish sounds will give rise to an amazing variety of fish imitations.

Deep Sea Fishing

The excitement generated by fishing games has always been as great as the frustration of waiting for a turn at the pole. Diminish the waiting time, and the game is immediately improved. Here is a version of this popular game that will absorb, challenge, and continue to entertain the children.

Materials: Dowels or sticks 2–3 feet in length; string; S-hook; packages of kitchen sponges; pipe cleaners; felt-tip pen; plastic bag.

To make the fishing rods: Tie a string to one end of the stick or dowel; secure the line by wrapping it around the pole and gluing if necessary. Attach an S-hook (heavy enough to hold the line straight down) to the other end of the line. The finished length of the line should be 2–3 feet.

To make the fish: Draw the whale, fish, dolphin, wave, and coral shapes on cardboard, following Figure G. Adjust so that the size of the "fish" does not exceed the size of the sponges you have purchased for the project. Cut out. Trace the animal pattern on the surface of the sponge using a felt-tip pen. The sponges should be fresh from the package since the moisture will make

Figure G

them easier to cut. Carefully cut the figure out of the sponge. Save the scraps to use for smaller fish, rocks, etc., made following the same procedure. Then pierce the larger figures with a pipe cleaner tied into a loop, which the children will try to catch on their hook (see Figure H). There should be enough sponge animals so that each child can fish at least 3 out during the game. The remaining smaller sponge figures should be put into a plastic bag.

To play the game: Children hold their rods and simply try to catch the fish by hooking the pipe-cleaner loop on their hook. The "fish" can be on the ground or in a pool of water. At the end of the game, the "catch of the day" should be added to the collection in the plastic bag, along with a note explaining their use in paint-printing projects. (Dip in paint, then print shape on paper). Send these bags home with the children at the end of the party. (Note that sponge paint printing can also be a project at the party. See "Alternatives" under the Seascapes project.)

Blow Boats

It will be smooth sailing for the children as they blow tiny sailboats across tabletops or along the floor. The race is on!

Materials: Paper egg cartons; craft pipe cleaners; clear Con-Tact paper; glue; construction paper; blue and white poster paint (optional).

To make sail patterns: Trace the smaller solid triangle to make the sail pattern and the larger triangle to make the sail cover pattern from Figure I; cut out. Use these paper patterns as templates for the sails.

To make individual boats: Using the templates, trace and cut out a construction-paper sail and clear Con-Tact paper sail cover. Decorate the sail with the child's name. Peel the backing off the sail cover, and affix the sail to one-half; affix

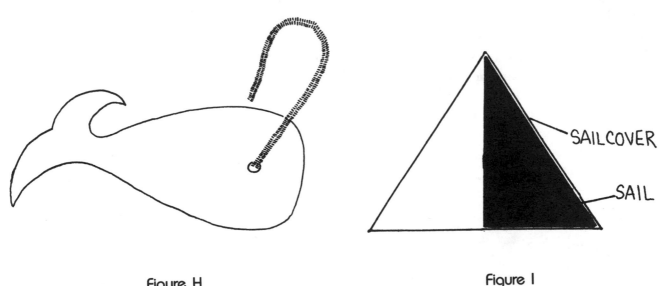

Figure H

Figure I

Alternative: Cut the forms from poster board and lace with a pipe cleaner pushed through a slit in the form. Recommend that the children use these figures to create a mobile at home.

the pipe cleaner along the midline of the sail cover; wrap the exposed, sticky side of the sail cover around the pipe cleaner, match up the edges, and stick to the exposed side of the sail. For the boat,

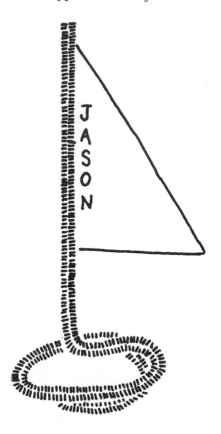

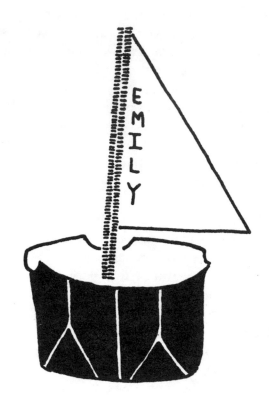

Figure J

cut out individual egg nest from egg carton and trim the edge. If you want to paint your boats, paint the inside white and the outside blue. Let dry. To insert the sail, curl the bottom of the pipe cleaner twice around as shown in Figure J, bending the mast into an upright position. The sail should clear the boat by about ¼ inch. Glue the pipe cleaner into place in the bottom of the boat by squirting some glue around the bottom, inside edges of the boat.

To play the game: Prepare for the races by cleaning a smooth surface large enough for at least 2 children in each heat of the race. A short period of experimentation before the race begins will allow children to develop the expertise to send their boats whizzing by blowing at the base of the boat. A room full of children inching their way across the floor blowing boats is a funny sight, and fun for them as well.

 Seascape

Children enjoy exercising their imagination. This creative project takes them into the mysterious world of underwater life, using recognizable, lovable creatures. Out of this fantasy they make a window decoration, wall hanging, necklace, or magnet . . . whatever form you choose.

Materials: Colored cellophane (light colors); scraps of poster board, colored papers, felts; sequins, confetti, glitter; pieces of evergreen; swatches of netting from potato bags or netting fabric; yarn for window decoration or necklace, magnetic tape for magnets; hole puncher; clear Con-Tact paper. (If Con-Tact paper is unavailable, glue pieces on poster board and cover in cellophane taped or glued on poster board.)

To make the patterns: Trace or draw the sea creatures in Figure K on paper; cut out. (For 6-inch window discs, these animals should be 1–3 inches, for necklaces and magnets 1–2 inches, for wall hangings any size.) Transfer the cutout patterns for the whale, octopus, rock, and little fish onto cardboard, tracing along the outline; cut

out. Use these cardboard pieces and the remaining paper pieces as templates for seascape components.

For each seascape: Using the templates, trace and cut out sea creatures in bright colors of felt and poster board. The cutouts must be 2-sided— i.e., they must have the finished appearance on

Figure K

both front and back. Cut proportionally small rocks and coral from felt and papers, and swatches of netting. For all projects, cut squares of Con-Tact paper and colored cellophane, slightly larger than the finished piece will be. (If Con-Tact paper is unavailable, cut a finished-size piece of poster board for the base.)

For each child: Put a complete set of precut animals, sequins, netting, glitter wrapped in a piece of plastic and/or confetti, and pieces of greenery in a plastic bag, with a base piece of Con-Tact paper.

To make: Help the children peel the backing off the Con-Tact paper. Place the paper sticky side up on the table, turning the corners under to secure the paper in place. Children simply stick their creatures and other decorations on the working surface to create a scenic picture. (If a poster-board base is substituted for a Con-Tact paper base, provide glue. Allow the assembled scenes to dry before moving to the next step.) When the children are finished, an adult puts a piece of cellophane on top of the picture, smooths it out, and trims the edges to the desired size. For necklaces and window decorations, punch a hole at the top and lace a piece of yarn through it; for magnets, attach a piece of magnetic tape to the back of the collage as inconspicuously as possible; for wall hangings, punch holes at the corners of the collage and the poster-board backing and tie the collage to the backing with yarn. Have an example of the finished product available for the children to see while they are doing the project.

Alternatives: A simple alternative to this project is to make the deep sea fishing treats as sponges (discussed earlier in this chapter) and use them for a sponge art project. Dip the sponges in paint and make prints with them on white or blue poster board. This requires that the deep sea fishing game precede the art project.

Whale Cake

The children will greet a blue whale cake with amusement and fellow feeling.

Materials: One 9 x 13-inch cake (see Cake Tips in "How to Use This Book"); 1 can or batch of white frosting; blue food color; red shoestring licorice, red rope licorice, Skittles, one black jelly bean, and miniature marshmallows.

To finish the cake: Following the pattern in Figure L, draw a full-sized pattern for the cake pieces on paper; cut out. Lay the 3 paper pattern pieces directly on the cake. Cut the cake with a large, sharp knife, keeping the knife as vertical as possible while cutting. Tint the frosting with blue food coloring. Assemble the cake by "gluing" the pieces together with frosting, according to Figure M (see page 92). Frost the cake on the sides and top with the blue icing. Add a rope licorice mouth, black jelly bean eye encircled with red Skittles, shoestring licorice finlike details, and a spout of shoestring licorice topped with miniature marshmallows, as in Figure M. Chocolate base candies can be substituted for the licorice/jelly/fruit types. In this case, use pretzel sticks in the spout and peanuts for the mouth.

Suggestions

Elaborating on this party theme with commercially available products is quite simple. The animal set involves a number of extremely lovable creatures, many of which are the subject of children's books. Coloring books with a scientific slant— covering a marine biologist's dream's array of aquatic life—are sold at many museums and zoos, as well as bookstores. Shells are sold in many stores; to a certain extent, however, this is geographical. (People living on the coasts will find such things more widely available.) Many stationers carry paper products adorned with drawings and pictures of shells. Soaps and chocolates are made in the shape of shells. The boat motif is also widely used in children's toys, books, craft products. If the party takes on a seasonal slant, summer products such as inexpensive beach or sand toys, balls, etc., are available. In any case, bath toys often follow the theme of this party quite nicely. Wind-up water toys, boats, bubble baths in fish containers, etc., are available year round.

If the party is held outdoors and water is involved, many people will find the entertainment takes care of itself. Be careful, however, that your paper products do not get wet and children do not spoil their favors. If the party is outdoors and water is involved, the substitution of the sponge prints for the seascapes is most sensible. The children can simply be hosed down after painting, as can their work area. Please be conscious of the fact that a party involving water requires much greater supervision. It will be easy to encourage parents to stay on a nice day, since an outdoor picnic atmosphere is by nature less exclusive. Fishing games can then be played with sponges in a rubber pool for heightened realism.

In any event, this is a lighthearted party that should be immensely enjoyed by all.

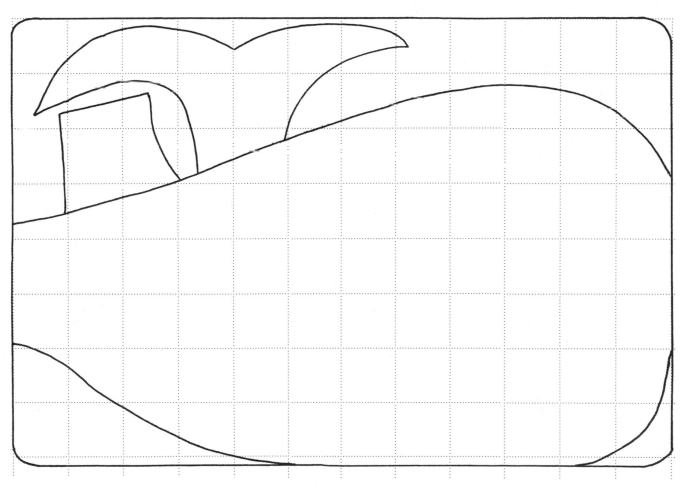

Figure L (1 sq. = 1 in.)

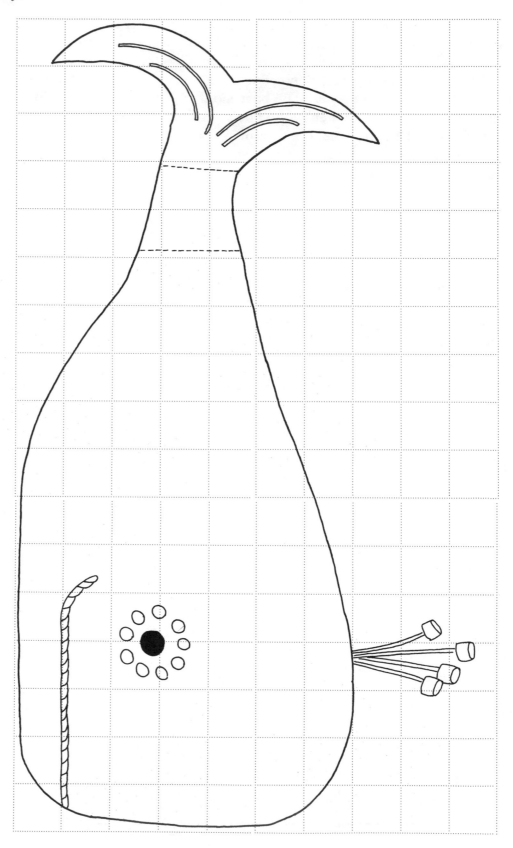

Figure M (1 sq. = 1 in.)

COOKIES, COOKIES, COOKIES

AGE GROUP

4 to 7 years old

PARTY LENGTH

1½ hours

You don't have to be a cookie monster to enjoy this party . . . but, it certainly doesn't hurt! For this celebration, the party goers take on the guise of minichefs and turn a luscious batch of cookie dough into scrumptious, crazy-looking cookies. It's a fun, creative, and festive way to make birthday dreams come true.

 The Plan

Announce the party by sending each child "Cookie," a paper, cookie-cutter cutout invitation—"ready to decorate" with sequins, fabric scraps, and colorful paper included—or by itself with the simple message, "Decorate me please!" Secure a piece of magnetic tape on the back, and "Cookie" doubles as a magnet.

Begin the party with a search for the missing cookie cutters. When they find them, have the children proceed with cookie cutters in hand to a table set for a hands-on cookie-making experience! Besides the essential dough and implements, give the children the fabulously fun and puffy Chef's Hats and Aprons—not your standard variety, but the perfect costume for the occasion and simply irresistible!

You can make the dough itself from scratch or a mix, or simply cut it from store-bought refrigerator dough. After the minichefs complete their creations and while the cookies are baking, have them play a few rounds of Catch the Cookie Monster and then send them off to the table, chanting, "We want cookies, we want cookies!" Follow their chanting with the traditional birthday song and a very untraditional dessert—a Gigantic, Pizza-Pan Cookie, decorated on top like a cake! Each child is given a slice or, even easier, a hand-served chunk of cookie! When the "monsters" have finished devouring the last of the crumbs, give them their own cookie creations—now cooled—plus an assortment of goodies for adding the final touches—frosting, sprinkles, chocolate chips, raisins, the works! Their completed creations will not only be food for consumption, they'll be their entries for the Bake Off. And in this contest, everyone wins! A judge (yourself or a helper) announces the award-winning cookies with a category to fit each, e.g., most colorful, most decorated, funniest, most beautiful, gooeyest, etc. Pin each minichef with a Cookie-Making Medal of Excellence. Each child will depart with great pride, dressed for the part and carrying away the sweets of success!

"Cookie" Cutout Invitation

"Cookie" comes ready to decorate and bearing the news of a party that would delight any cookie monster. This cookie is not edible, but the ones at the party will be. Magnetic "Cookie" will be around long after the party is over, sticking to the refrigerator and never getting stale!

Materials: Brown or other color poster board (1 sheet for every 20 invitations); white paper for the party information; glue; magnetic tape (available in hardware stores); small wiggle eyes; decorative items: ribbon, fabric scraps, buttons, sequins, rickrack, or other remnants; small plastic bags; envelopes.

To make the pattern: Trace the outline of the cookie shown in Figure A or trace around your own favorite gingerbread cookie cutter on paper; cut out. Transfer the cutout pattern onto cardboard; cut out. Use this cardboard piece as the template for making "Cookie."

For each invitation: Trace around the template on poster board and on a white sheet of paper; cut out. Leaving the head blank, write the party information on the white cutout: Glue this cutout onto the poster-board cutout, lining up the edges. Cut a ¾-inch piece of magnetic tape and affix it to "Cookie's" head on the white side. Gather the decorative items, such as the ones shown in Figure A, and place them in the plastic bag, along with a brief note to use the pieces for decorating "Cookie," who then turns into a magnet!

Text: Hey good lookin', want to come cookin'? Join us for (child's name)'s birthday bake off./ Date, Time, Place, R.S.V.P. Wear washable clothes./ Decorate "Cookie," then stick him on your refrigerator—he has a "magnetic" personality!

 # Four-Star Chef's Hat

This highly rated hat will make a championship baker out of anyone who wears it. Because it is made with an elasticized headband, it fits every head with ease.

Materials: White poster board (1 sheet for every 13 hats); package of white crepe paper (1 package for every 2 hats); fine-tip marking pen or crayon; white thread or glue; transparent tape; hole puncher; round-cord elastic; white cloth tape (available at hardware stores, optional).

To make each hat: Cut out a 3 x 18-inch strip of poster board for the headband. Using a marking pen or crayon, print or write the guest's name, e.g., Chef Peter, in the center of the headband.

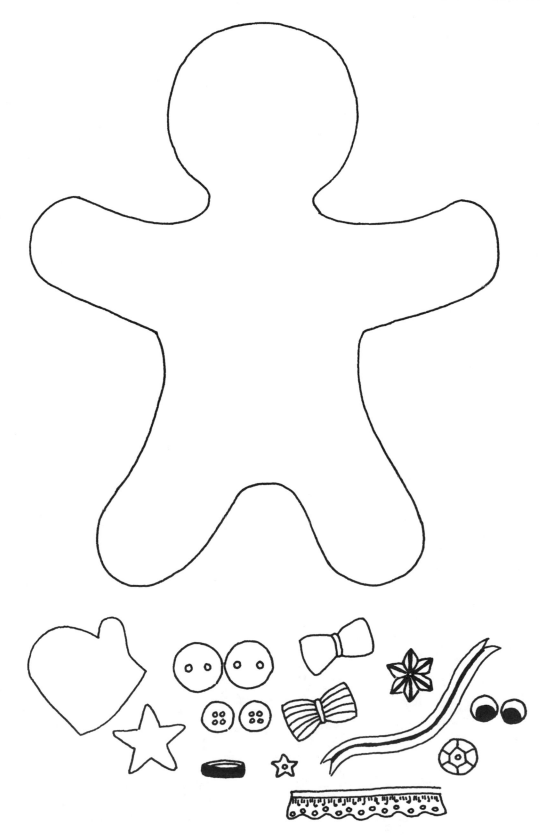

figure A

Cut a length of crepe paper 20 x 44 inches long (this generally is half of the sheet that comes in the package). Fold the paper in half lengthwise and machine stitch or glue together along one long edge, as shown in Figure B. Lay the piece flat on a table. Measure and mark the unstitched edges: beginning at one edge, measure in 4 inches from the stitching line and mark this point "A"; do the same for the opposite edge, marking that point "E"; mark the top edge at the "fold" letter "C." Find the midpoint between letters "A" and "C" and mark it "B" (so that along the edges "A" to "B" equals "B" to "C"); do the same for "E" and "C" and mark this midpoint "D," as shown in Figure B. Measure and mark the headband: locate the midpoint, 9 inches in from the end, and mark this point "C"; measure in 2 inches from the end of the headband on both sides, mark one point "A" and the other "E"; find the midpoint between "A" and "C" and mark it "B"; find the midpoint between "C" and "E" and mark it "D," as shown in Figure C. Turn the crepe paper

right side out, with the seam to the inside. Line up the markings on the crepe paper with those on the headband ("A" with "A," "B" with "B," etc.), so that the wrong side of the band slightly overlaps the right side of the crepe paper. Tape together at these markings. Gather up the "dangling" crepe paper between the markings, treating the corners as if they were straight edges. To gather it, simply bunch it up with your fingers and finger-press the folds in place; tape the gathered edge to the hat, working from "C" to "B" to "A," and then from "C" to "D" to "E." There will be approximately 8 inches of crepe-paper edge unsecured in the back (see Figure C); this is hidden

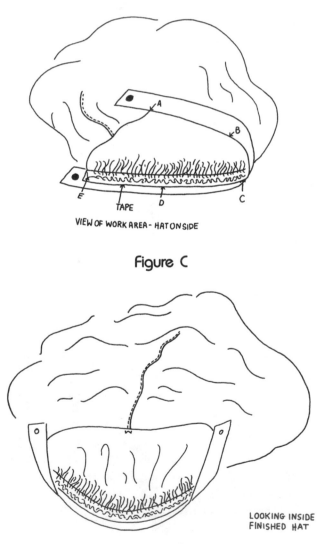

VIEW OF WORK AREA - HAT ON SIDE

Figure C

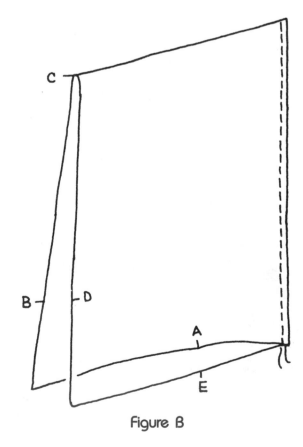

Figure B

LOOKING INSIDE
FINISHED HAT

Figure D

in the voluminous folds in the hat when it is worn and is essential for a proper fit. See Figure D. To complete, place a length of cloth tape over the transparent tape, if desired, for a smoother finish and neater appearance. Punch holes at the ends of the band and tie together with a 6-inch piece of round-cord elastic. A front view of the completed hat is shown in Figure E.

> NOTE: This hat appears complex at first, especially because you have to treat the hat edge from "A" to "E" as if it were one continuous, straight edge (when there really are 2 corners). But if you keep this in mind, you'll find after you put 1 hat together, the rest are a snap! And the finished product will reward you many times over for your effort—it is truly special!

Figure E

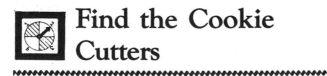

Find the Cookie Cutters

This hunt gets the party rolling and the spirits cooking! Before the party, hide several cookie cutters for each child in 2 or more rooms, if possible. At party time, send the children off in all directions—with bags in hand—in search of the much needed cookie cutters. When found, gather all the children around the table to start the cookie-making brigade.

Cookie-Making Brigade

Here's where the fun really begins. Each child puts on his or her own personalized Chef's Hat and Apron (as discussed in this chapter) and creates a batch of cookies with the new-found cookie cutters!

Materials: Cookie dough; cookie cutters; cookie sheets; waxed paper; spatulas for lifting the cookies onto the cookie sheets.

Before the party: Make enough batches of cookie dough from your own recipe or a mix, or use purchased refrigerator dough, so that each child can make at least 6 cookies. Roll the dough onto individual sheets of waxed paper, cut for each child. Purchased dough can be laid out sliced and then flattened by the child's hand at party time (or you can roll the slices together as for regular cookie dough). Cover and store the dough, stacked one on top of the other in the refrigerator.

At party time: Uncover each rolled-out dough section and place it on a table or other comfortable, kid-oriented work surface. A large sheet of plywood could be placed on cinderblocks and covered with a plastic cloth. Using this work surface, the children can simply kneel on the floor and easily get their hands (and more!) into the dough. Be sure to allow enough room for each child to work easily. Then let the children "go to town" with the dough and cutters (see Figure F, page 98). Once the cookies are completed, you and a helper can place them on cookie sheets prepared with narrow strips of waxed paper marked with each child's initials for easy identification of the cookies. Bake the cookies and then place them on racks to cool (see Figure G, page 98).

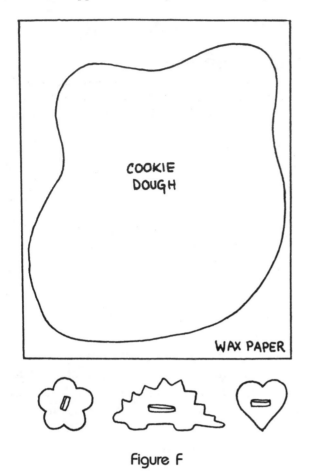

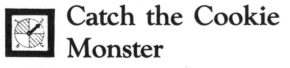

Figure F

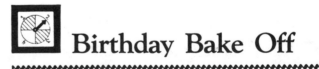

Figure G

Catch the Cookie Monster

This is a fun game to play while the cookies are baking and cooling. It helps the children to let off a little steam!

One child is "It." (The birthday child should be first.) He or she counts to 5, and everyone else scatters. "It" tries to catch a cookie monster. Whoever is caught becomes "It." This game needs plenty of space and is ideally played outdoors. For a less active game, draw a crazy face resembling a cookie monster on a paper plate and have the children pass it around while music plays; whoever has the plate when the music stops has caught the cookie monster. Continue with this sequence until each child has a turn catching the monster or until their interest subsides. The same game can be played with a balloon that has been decorated with marking pens. Instead of passing the balloon, they toss it to the next person!

Birthday Bake Off

The Bake Off is a contest that applauds the culinary accomplishments of the minichefs. Have each child pick out his favorite cookie as his entry. Line the cookies up and announce one by one the awards for the cookies, so that each child is a winner—most colorful, prettiest, funniest, most decorated, gooeyest, etc. Pin a Medal of Excellence (discussed later in this chapter) on each chef and end with a rousing round of applause. Wrap the cookies in tissue paper, bakery-fashion, and place in a name-labeled bag for the children to take home (see Figure H).

Just be sure to have some moist, disposable towelettes and a garbage bag close at hand!

Figure H

![cookie-decorating icon] **Cookie-Decorating Brigade**

This cookie-decorating session takes the cookie that each child has made into the realm of birthday fantasy. Each child can be as creative as he or she likes, wielding colored frostings, sprinkles, candies, and goodies of all kinds. The sky's the limit!

Before the party, fill paper bowls or cupcake tins for each child with colored frosting, sprinkles, rainbow nonpareils, etc.; then fill 1 bowl with an assortment of candies, raisins, marshmallows, and other goodies for each child. Provide craft sticks, tongue depressors, and/or spoons for applying the frosting (see Figure I). Have all this, plus the appropriate cookies, assembled at each child's place at the table and give the go-ahead! Don't be surprised if some of the goodies end up in the stomachs and on the faces—it's part of the fun.

Figure I

 # Chef's Apron

Every 4-star chef deserves a great-looking apron. Here's one that's as easy-as-pie to make out of fuss-free felt. There's no sewing required at all!

Materials: Blue felt for the apron (1 yard of 72-inch-wide felt for every 7 aprons); white felt for the decorative hat (¼ yard for 7); scraps or squares of felt for the stars in purple, pink, red, and green; glue or fusible webbing.

To make the pattern: Draw the outline of the apron (including the neck opening), hat, and hat band and 1 complete star, as shown in Figure J, on paper; cut out.

To make each apron: Pin the paper patterns onto the felt—apron on blue, hat pieces on white, and star on 4 different-colored felt pieces—and cut out. Lay the apron out flat. Center and position the chef's hat pieces on the front of the bib, placing the band approximately 2¾ inches up from the bottom edge and the hat ¼ inch from the top of the band. Glue, or fuse in place using fusible webbing and following manufacturer's directions. Position the 4 stars on the band and glue or fuse in place (see Figure J). Slip the apron over the chef's head, and he or she is ready to bake up a storm!

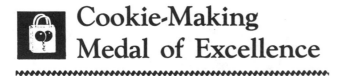 # Cookie-Making Medal of Excellence

The cookie-making medal makes a proud winner out of each party participant. It looks quite official in all its shininess and stripes, but each one takes only a minute or 2 to make.

Materials: Foil cupcake tins; ¾-inch striped ribbon; double-stick tape; safety pins.

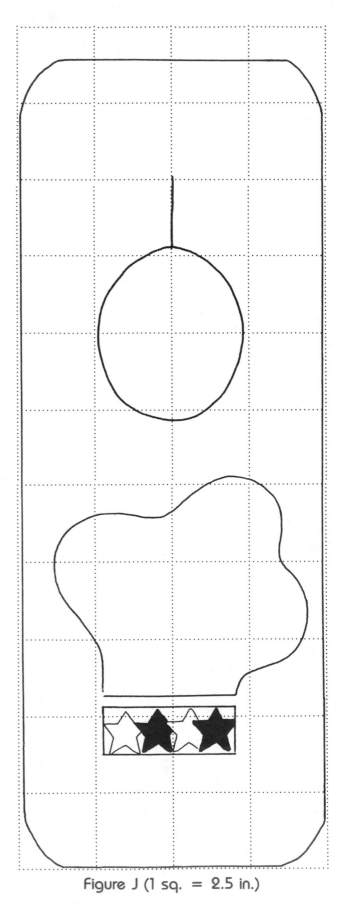

Figure J (1 sq. = 2.5 in.)

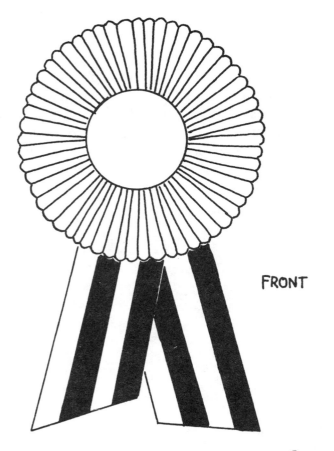
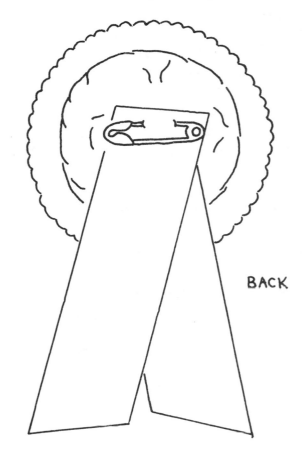

FRONT

BACK

Figure K

To make each medal: Simply flatten out the cupcake tin so that the ridged section forms a "halo" around the bottom round section (see front view, Figure K). Cut a 4-inch piece of ribbon, fold in half, and trim the ends on the diagonal. Tape the folded edge to the back of the flattened tin, using double-stick tape. Add a safety pin for securing the medal on the winner (see back view, Figure K), and *voilá*, you have the Medal of Excellence.

 # Gigantic, Pizza-Pan Cookie

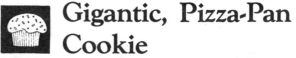

This monstrous morsel takes the place of a cake for this cookie, "kooky" party.

Materials: Two batches of cookie dough made from a mix or from scratch, or 1 extra-large, family-size package of refrigerator dough; pizza pan; wax paper; vegetable shortening for greasing the pan; 1 can of frosting; 1 tube of decorating gel for the writing; candies for decorating—spice drops, watermelon slices, jelly circles, licorice logs, lifesavers.

To make the cookie cake: Spread the cookie dough in the pizza pan to fill it; if using refrigerator dough, simply slice it and place the slices side by side in the pan. Bake the cookie as usual, until brown (this will take a little longer than with smaller cookies), in a well-greased, wax-paper-lined, shallow pizza pan. Cool about 10 minutes before carefully removing the cookie from the pan. Decorate as desired with frosting and goodies. Write in the birthday message with the decorating gel (see Figure L). At party time, place lifesavers wherever you want to put candles—these will hold the candles on the cookie! Put the candles in, light them, and sing. Then let the children break off a chunk of cookie (or you do it) to munch in celebration.

Alternatives: For a very large crowd (or if you want leftovers), you can make 2 cookies and spread softened ice cream in between for a jumbo cookie/creamwich! Or, for a store-bought approach, why not simply buy individual cookie/creamwiches for the children?

party-time baking. For the contest, the awards could be given for the group.

If you give this party in its complete form, be sure to have extra help—a couple of adults or favorite baby-sitters. Someone needs to watch the cookies as they bake, and depending on the size of the party, 2 or more helpers can put the children's cookies on the cookie sheets. And, of course, the dough and the decorations have to be set up! It's worth it!

Suggestions

For very young children, 3 or 4 prebaked, pizza-pan cookies can be used for decorating as a group, eliminating the cookie-dough phase. It's just as much fun and extremely easy since it requires no

Figure L

JUNGLE SAFARI

```
AGE GROUP
4 to 7 years old
~~~~~~~~~~~~~~~~~~
PARTY LENGTH
1½ to 2 hours
```

The universality of animal appeal gives this party a basic energy and spiritedness that will captivate any child. Add to this an exotic environment and adventure, and you have a sure-fire formula for a successful party.

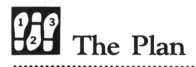 The Plan

The animal mood of the party is set when the child receives the invitation, a simple-to-make Swinging Monkey Magnet to hang on the refrigerator. The day of the party your house is ready to be transformed into an Instant Jungle: have the children create a vivid, textured scene with bright tissue flowers, paper grasses, leaves, and other colorful gobbledygook. Instant Jungle is instant satisfaction. Adventure comes next in the form of a Safari. You choose the safari style that best suits your needs. Children will naturally respond to the grand hunt for wild animals, whether simple or elaborate.

Exhausted by the big chase, the children will be in need of refreshments. A picnic-style setting on the floor (or table) is perfect for the party foods. The Jungle Bird Hats brighten the setting. While the food is being served, children will enjoy games of Follow the Leader (echoing animal noises) and Animal Telephone (whispering animal noises or animal names around the circle). When you bring out the Elephant Cake, excitement will peak.

Refreshed, the children return to party games. Focus their attention with several rounds of Animal Charades. The more structured activity of creating new species of Mix and Match Animals is a natural follow-up to charades. Thinking of new names for their new animals ("Jane's zeonphant") will be as crazy as making the animals themselves. End the party with a series of games called Lion and Tiger Tamers, using yellow and orange balloons, that will guarantee the children will be collected, happy, and amused when the parents arrive. Decorate the children with Animal Faces, using costume face makeup, as a parting gift, and send them on their way.

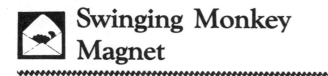

Swinging Monkey Magnet

Monkey business is the name of the game at your child's party, so it is only appropriate to send out this message loud and clear. The monkey is a magnet that will turn your young friend's refrigerator into an eventful reminder of the party day.

Materials: Brown and green poster board (1 sheet of each for 14 invitations); magnetic tape (available in hardware stores); paper clasp; envelopes.

To make pattern: Trace the leaf and the single monkey (monkey #1) shown in Figure A on paper; cut out. Transfer the cutout patterns onto cardboard, drawing along the outlines; cut out. Use these cardboard pieces as templates for the monkey invitation.

For each invitation: Using the template, trace 2 monkeys on brown poster board; cut out. Ap-

ply the magnetic tape vertically on the head of one monkey (monkey #1); the other monkey will be the swinging monkey (monkey #2). Using the template, trace a leaf on green poster board; cut out. Print the invitation text on one side of the leaf. Punch a hole in the right leg of the magnet monkey (monkey #1) and the left arm of the swinging monkey (monkey #2), as shown in Figure A. Punch a hole at the base of the leaf. Match up the holes in all 3 pieces and insert the paper clasp. The lower monkey should swing freely. Test to see if the magnet is strong enough. If it isn't, simply add another piece of magnetic tape to the body of monkey #1.

Alternatives: Postcards picturing wild animals (lions, zebras, etc.) make an excellent invitation to this party. Photographs from a zoo trip or cut from a nature magazine and glued to a square piece of drawing paper or poster board with the invitation text written on the back are another alternative. Realistic designs or pictures are the key to creating the sense of adventure.

Text: It's a jungle out there!/Come explore it at (child's name)'s birthday party!/Date, Time, Place, R.S.V.P.

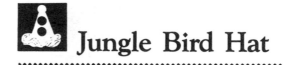

Jungle Bird Hat

Transform the children into birds of flight with this simply designed bird hat.

Materials: Colorful poster board—purple, red, pink, orange, blue (1 sheet for 3 hats); yellow, white, and black Con-Tact paper (or construction paper); round-cord elastic; hole puncher.

To make the pattern: Trace the outline of the eye white, eye center, beak, and hat (one-half of the finished hat) shown in the pattern section at the back of the book on a large piece of paper. Trace a mirror-image of the half-bird drawing to complete the other half of the hat. Cut out.

MONKEY #1

MONKEY #2 →

Figure A

Figure B

Transfer cutout patterns for the eye parts and beak onto cardboard, and the bird hat onto poster board, drawing along the outlines; cut out. Use these pieces as the templates for making the hats.

For each hat: Using the template, trace a hat on poster board; cut out. Using the templates, trace 2 eye whites on white Con-Tact paper, 2 eyeballs on black Con-Tact paper, and 1 beak on yellow Con-Tact paper; cut out. Affix the eye white to the hat, the eyeball on the eye white, and the beak to the hat, according to the pattern. Punch holes near the ends of the hat and tie with round-cord elastic to fit. A constructed hat is shown in Figure B.

Instant Jungle

"Jungle" translates into "nature gone wild" in the minds of children. Creating that overgrown, colorful environment is one way to involve them in developing the party concept. Two projects allow them to construct the jungle; one version becomes a picture for their wall, the other the scenery for the party.

NOTE: Your safari choice will affect your choice in Instant Jungle and the scheduling of party events.

Materials: Version I and II—bright colored tissue papers, poster boards, construction papers, crepe papers, etc., and scraps. Version I only—masking tape. Version II only—black or other (not green) colored poster board (1 for 2 or 3 jungle boards); green poster board; plastic wiggle eyes; glue; (optional) corrugated cardboard.

Version I: "Decorate the House." Well in advance of the party make large boxes of brightly colored tissue-paper flowers, construction paper or poster-board spirals, leaves, grasses, crunched-up balls of tissue paper, animal cutouts, etc. (see Figure C). They should measure 4–8 inches. Put them in cartons. Also have strips of crepe paper and streamers on hand. The children will stick these items on a wall or mantel. Select a site. If you are using a wall and are nervous about using masking tape on the paint, hang brown wrapping paper for the children to tape their decorations on. (Wrapping paper is a partial solution but will itself have to be securely hung with tape). When the children arrive at the party instruct them to decorate the selected area. Assign an adult to roll the masking tape for the children until the project is over. Have enough decorations on hand so that the end product is a densely decorated area. This is a perfect backdrop for your party photographs.

Version II: "Jungle Boards." Well in advance of the party make brightly colored tissue-paper flowers, construction paper or poster-board spirals, grasses, leaves, animal figures, flowers (see Figure C), and crushed tissue-paper balls. They should be roughly 2–5 inches in size and in sufficient quantity to densely cover the jungle boards. The size of the jungle boards is flexible, although it should be noted that half a poster board (14 x 22 inches) or a large piece of construction paper would be the most convenient sizes. Cut pieces of corrugated cardboard to the size you have chosen, 1 per child, and cover them with brightly colored poster board or construction paper. Glue colored covering in place and trim. For a "jungle at night" effect (shown in Figure D), with eyes peering out of the darkness, cover with black

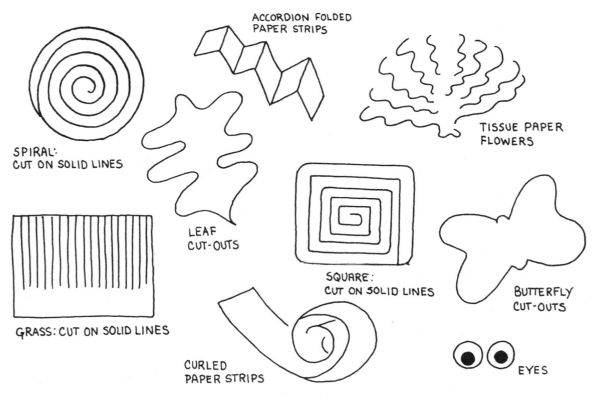

SPIRAL:
CUT ON SOLID LINES

ACCORDION FOLDED
PAPER STRIPS

TISSUE PAPER
FLOWERS

LEAF
CUT-OUTS

SQUARE:
CUT ON SOLID LINES

BUTTERFLY
CUT-OUTS

GRASS: CUT ON SOLID LINES

CURLED
PAPER STRIPS

EYES

Figure C

Figure D

poster board. Glue a strip of green poster board textured to look like grass across the bottom third of the board. Put the premade decorations, plus some purchased plastic wiggle eyes, in plastic bags, 1 bag per child, and label them "Instant Jungle." Distribute the boards and the bags when the children are seated at the project table. Give each child a glue pad (a small square of cardboard with a blob of white glue) and a glue stick to spread it with (a cotton swab without the cotton). Have children decorate their jungle boards, hang them on the walls for party decoration, and take them home when the party ends.

Suggestions: Sources of free, colorful paper are tissue paper from the dry cleaners, vegetable grocers, etc., and solid-colored, decorative paper bags. Kleenex is also good material to use for tissue flowers.

The Safari

A safari, simple or elaborate, will turn this party into an adventure. Several alternative safaris are presented below, each with its own excitement.

Safari 1: The simplest safari consists of a hunt where children find hidden plastic animals or clothespin animals (described later in this chapter).

Safari 2: An elaborate hunt where children find hidden stuffed animals and return them to a "zoo" or "game preserve" (a playpen or decorated refrigerator box) becomes a fast-paced game when children receive stickers, plastic animals, small stuffed animals, or felt animals in exchange for each animal they capture.

Safari 3: A safari in which children track animals is exceptionally fun. To prepare for this safari, rolls of adding machine tape and a children's animal or letter stamp set are required. Stencils may

be used in place of stamps. For each child, a strip of adding machine tape 50+ feet in length is stamped with figures or letters to form a trail. The strip should be stamped roughly every 10–20 inches for its entire length. To make each child's trail unique, use different stamps and different color ink pads. Starting the trails in different locations, tape the strips along walls, over and under furniture, and in and out of closets the morning of the party. At the end of each trail, put an animal theme treat (plastic animal, small stuffed animal, inflatable animal, animal crackers or cookies, clothespin animals, animal postcards, animal magazine, etc.). At safari time each child follows a set of tracks to the end of the trail to capture a treat. Choosing this tracking safari means that the safari space cannot be entered by the children until the hunt begins and that the instant jungle activity space cannot overlap. This will affect the order in which you schedule the activities.

To make stencils: If you do not own or cannot borrow stamp sets, follow Figure E to create simple stencils from cardboard. Draw the animal on the board and cut out in a single cut, starting from the edge of the piece and following the outline of the animal. Tape the segment from the edge of the cardboard to the edge of the animal closed. Add simple details to the animals as you stencil on the adding machine tape.

Follow the Leader (Monkey See, Monkey Do) and Animal Telephone

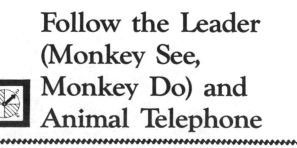

Play a game of Follow the Leader in which the leader pretends to be an animal of his or her choice. Give all the children a chance to be leader by making the turns short. A boisterous version of this game can be played sitting down where

Figure E

the children select an animal sound and the others imitate. For a quieter version, play Animal Telephone. As in the classic telephone game, one child begins by whispering to the person sitting next to him or her the name of an animal or an animal sound. The message is whispered around the circle and surprisingly modified. Encouraged to use complicated names and silly sounds, children will find that many animals are known to other children that they never even knew existed!

Animal Charades

Take the performance anxiety out of charades by playing team animal charades. Divide the children into several groups (minimum 4 children per group) and have all the members of a particular team pretend to be an animal while the other teams try to guess. Before they begin, show the team acting out the charade a picture of the animal to avoid confusion over what animal they are acting out. Use animals that are easier to guess (lion, monkey, elephant, crocodile-alligator, giraffe, pig). When the audience teams guess the animal, give all the children a treat (plastic animal, sticker, candy, etc.). Try to put at least one "ham" on each team.

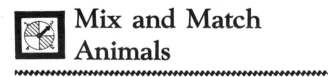

Mix and Match Animals

Create a zeaffant, a gironbra, a liafbra . . . funny animals from the wilderness of the imagination. In this game, children make funny animals by mixing up 3-piece puzzles of known wild animals.

Each child is given a complete animal (a lion, giraffe, zebra or elephant) in a bag. Children stand around a large table. To begin, they assemble their animal for all to see. Start playing music and instruct the children to walk around the table until the music stops. When the music stops and the children stop walking, have them pick up the head of the animal they are standing in front of and start the music again. When the music stops the second time, the children place the animal head on the animal in front of them. This accomplished, the music begins again, and the children start walking. When the music stops this time, the children are asked to take the legs of the animal in front of them. The music starts and stops again, and the children place the legs on the animal in front of them. One more round of music/walking determines which animal the child will call his or her own. The children are then asked to think of a name for their new animal. The new puzzle is then put in the bag with the child's and animal's name on it.

Suggestions: Decorating the game table with green crepe paper to look like grass adds to this game. Thoughtful music selections can increase the fun, too. (An excellent choice is "Aba Daba Honeymoon" found on "Sharon, Lois & Bram Singin' and Swingin'," a popular children's record).

Materials: Gold poster board or felt; white poster board; grey felt; brown and black markers; black or dark felt or paper; small bags.

To make the pattern: Following the drawings for each animal in Figures F–I, draw patterns for each animal on cardboard. Note that the proportions must be preserved for the animal parts to be interchangeable. To guarantee this, make a form for the neck cut and the body-leg separation that can be placed on every animal once made. The width of the animals' bodies must be identical. These puzzle cuts are indicated by the solid line in each figure.

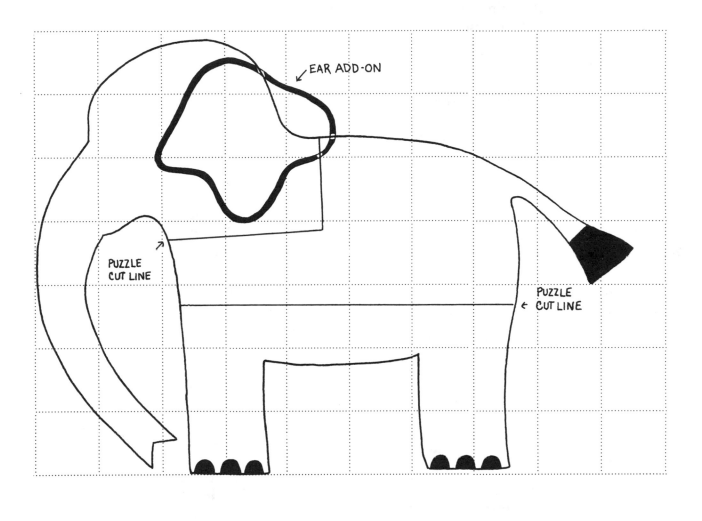

Figure F

To make the puzzles: Trace whole animal patterns on base of poster board; cut out (zebra and giraffe should be traced on white poster board, lion on gold poster board or any color if it is finished with gold felt, and elephant on any color of poster board.) Cut pieces of grey and gold felt larger than the elephant and lion base. Glue the animal form to the felt; let dry. Trim the felt to the edge of the form. Cut an ear for the elephant from black felt and glue to the animal along the long face edge only. The other side of the ear should be unattached. Color in the details on the giraffe with brown marker, and the zebra with black marker, as shown in Figures G and H. Rule lines on the back of the animals according to Figures F-I, using the form you have created in the pattern section. Cut along the lines as straight as possible, separating each animal into 3 segments. Be careful not to cut the elephant's ear! Place each animal in a bag, one for each child.

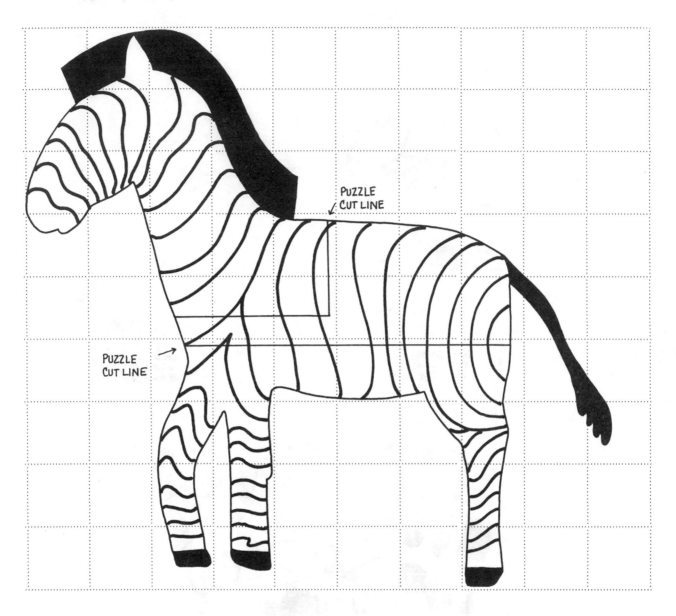

PUZZLE
CUT LINE

PUZZLE
CUT LINE

figure G

PUZZLE
CUT LINE

PUZZLE
CUT LINE →

Figure H

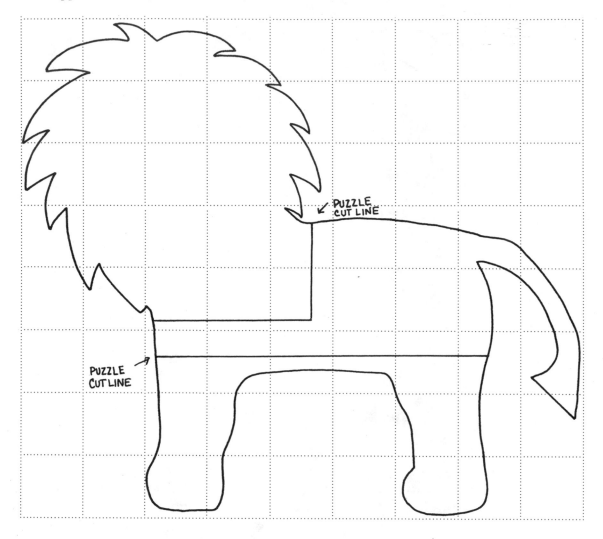

PUZZLE CUT LINE

PUZZLE CUT LINE

Figure 1

Lion and Tiger Tamers

Give your balloon games animal magnetism! Multitudes of yellow and orange balloons turn into a tangle of lions and tigers with children in hot pursuit.

Game I: Put a large number of balloons (at least 3 per child) on the floor of the room. Let the children wade through the balloons while you explain to them that the lions and tigers (represented by yellow and orange balloons) must be separated. If they can accomplish this within 30 seconds—putting the yellow balloons on one side of the room and the orange on the other—everyone will receive a treat. The children are fighting the clock. The amount of time that is reasonable depends on the number of children and the size of the room, so play it by ear.

Game II: Using the same balloons, explain to the children that their next task is to get the lions and tigers (balloons) off the floor—all at once! They can do this by sticking them on the wall with static electricity, holding them, stuffing them in their shirt, or setting them atop the furniture. Set a time limit and go.

Game III: A traditional race with balloons held between the legs is somewhat sillier when the children are convinced they are holding wild animals between their knees. Offer a treat to anyone who can cross the room successfully without dropping the balloon.

Game IV: Have children capture the wild animals by throwing them into a cage. Here the balloons are thrown into an open-top box from a prescribed distance. Give children treats after each successful throw, or after all the animals are captured.

Other balloon games: Any traditional balloon game can be simply modified to fit this format. Get into the spirit and create your own lion and tiger tamers!

 # Animal Faces

Using costume face makeup, give the children the animal look of their choice. Have more than one person making up the children so that they don't have to wait an eternity for their turn at the mirror.

Clothespin Animals

Searching out flocks and herds of exotic animals is great fun, and clothespin animals make ideal specimens.

Materials: Wooden clothespins (type pictured in Figure J); glue; for monkey, brown poster paint, thick brown or white pipe cleaners; for flamingo, pink poster paint, pink felt, white pipe cleaners; for giraffe, brown magic marker, white poster paint, tiny tubetini pasta; for zebra, white poster paint, black magic marker, black felt; for lion, extra-furry yellow pipe cleaner, yellow poster paint, black button thread; for tiger, orange paint, black marker, black button thread; for elephant, grey felt, grey poster paint, white pipe cleaner.

For all animals: Apply the base color paint (monkey—brown; flamingo—pink; giraffe—white; zebra—white; lion—yellow; tiger—orange; elephant—grey) and allow the clothespins to dry. An excellent place for this is on the rim of a glass.

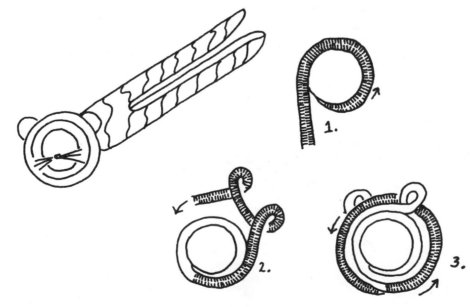

Figure J

To make tiger: With a black felt-tip pen, add stripes to clothespin, according to Figure J. Follow the pipe cleaner wrapping instructions shown in Figure J. (1) Wrap an orange pipe cleaner around neck once. (2) On the second wrap, add ears by twisting the pipe cleaner as shown. (3) On the third wrap, bring end between the ears, around the clothespin, and tuck the end in back. For the whiskers, take 3 strings of black coat-button thread and tie together in the middle with a fourth string. Trim on each side of the knot to a length of ¾ inch. Glue the knot to the face of the clothespin and let dry on the rim of a cup.

To make monkey: Follow the pipe cleaner wrapping instructions in Figure K for the ear details. (1) Wrap a beige pipe cleaner, with ears bent in, once around the neck of the brown clothespin. (2) Secure the configuration on the second wrap and tuck the end in. Add a second pipe cleaner for a tail, following Figure K. Bend the

tail into a wavy shape with a curl at the end; glue in place if necessary.

To make lion: Wrap 2 or 3 plush yellow pipe cleaners around the neck of the yellow clothespin so that the clothespin looks like the one shown in Figure L. Add whiskers made of black coat-button thread as described in the directions for making the tiger.

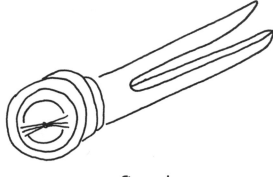

Figure L

To make elephant: Cut grey felt ears (1 piece), according to a pattern traced from Figure M, and

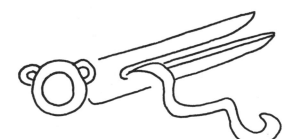

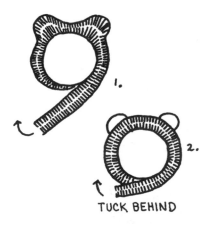

1.

2.

TUCK BEHIND

Figure K

glue to the neck of the grey clothespin. Let dry. Place the middle of a 5- or 6-inch length of white pipe cleaner around the nape of the neck, covering the point where the ears are glued on, and pinch together below the head. Twist the last 2 inches together and bend into a trunklike curve. Trim the end of the trunk to give it a finished look, as in Figure M.

To make zebra: Cut out 2 small black felt ears according to a pattern traced from Figure N. Draw stripes on white clothespin with a black felt-tip pen, according to Figure N. Glue on ears as shown.

To make flamingo: Cut 2 bright pink felt beaks using a pattern traced from Figure P. Glue the beak pieces together. While the glue is still moist, peel the face portion of the beaks apart and stick each side to the head of the pink clothespin, as shown in Figure P. Mold the beak to the face. Using 1 long pipe cleaner, add legs, as shown in Figure P.

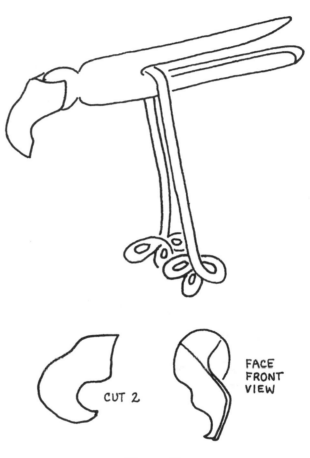

CUT 2

Figure N

To make giraffe: Following Figure O, draw brown spots on white clothespin, using a brown marker or felt-tip pen. Color tiny macaroni with some brown marker and glue macaroni onto head.

CUT 2

FACE FRONT VIEW

Figure P

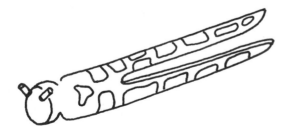

Figure O

Picnic Lunch

Lemonade, sandwiches, bowls of trail mix, peanuts, unusual fruits, and pineapple served on a tablecloth spread out on the floor will add reality to the safari. Serving lunch is not essential since a sensational elephant cake can stand on its own.

To prepare the pineapple: Quarter the pineapple lengthwise, cutting through the leaves. Leave them on as decoration. Core each quarter of the pineapple and separate the meat from the rind in a single piece. Slice once lengthwise and as many times crosswise as needed to make even, bite-sized pieces. Stick a miniature marshmallow on a furry cocktail toothpick, and stick that toothpick into a single piece of pineapple. Top every piece with a marshmallow toothpick, as shown in Figure Q.

Figure Q

Elephant Cake

This cake is incredibly easy to make and so in keeping with the party theme. Children really do love elephants.

Materials: One 9 x 13-inch cake (see Cake Tips in "How to Use This Book"); 1 can or batch of frosting; pink, grey, or blue food coloring; white, black, and one other color jelly beans; shoestring licorice.

To finish the cake: Following the pattern in Figure R, draw a full-size pattern for the cake pieces; cut out. Lay the paper pattern pieces directly on the cake and cut along the edges with a sharp, large kitchen knife, keeping it as vertical as possible when cutting. Tint the icing grey, blue, or pink. Glue the feet and trunk end in place with icing. Frost the assembled cake on the top and sides. Add the details, according to Figure S, to create white jelly bean toes, jelly bean–outlined ear, black jelly bean eye, white jelly bean tusk, frosting or clipped shoestring licorice wrinkles, and shoestring licorice tail.

Suggestions

There are many commercially available products that coordinate with this party—plastic animals, small clip-on animals, inflatable animals, animal crackers or cookies, postcards and stickers, animal nature magazines and books, posters, animal noses and other costume elements, pens and pencils with animal tops, plants, stamp sets that can be broken up and given out as individual favors, cookie cutters, knickknacks, whistles, and so on. Keep this in mind when buying treats, prizes, and favors for the party and when looking for substitutions for party elements described in this chapter.

Decorating the house has been made a party activity; however, party preparation can include hanging green streamers from the ceiling to give the look of grasses and overgrown vegetation.

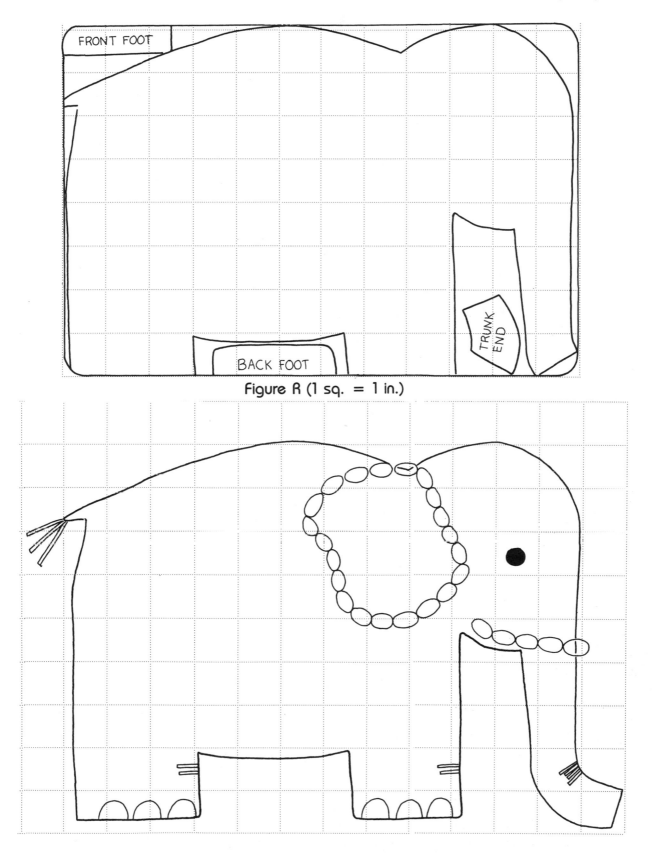

FRONT FOOT

BACK FOOT

TRUNK. END

Figure R (1 sq. = 1 in.)

Figure S (1 sq. = 1 in.)

10

MARVELOUS, MYSTERIOUS MAGIC PARTY

AGE GROUP

4 to 7 years old

PARTY LENGTH

1½ to 2 hours

A bit of abracadabra plus a trick or 2 up the sleeve are only the beginning of this very magical birthday celebration. The joy it evokes is no illusion. The greatest illusion, perhaps, is the magic the children themselves perform!

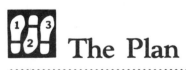 ## The Plan

Send the announcement of the magical event tucked into a paper magician's hat. When your guests slide the stick-puppet bunny up out of the hat, the message of the fun ahead is perfectly clear! While waiting for the magical day to arrive, the children can "perfect" their pop-up bunny trick.

At its magical best, this party makes each child feel as if he or she has his or her own special magic. As soon as they arrive, give each child a simple poster-board Wand, along with an assortment of decorative items—glitter, sequins, small felt shapes, paper cutouts, stickers—and glue. Their little hands get busy and before you know it, they transform their wands into their very own magical props! Then put the children into action by sending them on a hunt. It can be as simple as Finding the Missing Bunnies (paper) or pennies or peanuts for the magician's trick. Or it can be a treasure hunt with clues written or pictured on bunnies or hats, leading the children ultimately to a collection of easy-to-make Magician's Capes and Top Hats. Any way you do it, you're sure to generate excitement and fun.

As if by magic, the children are gathered together with capes and hats on, ready to experience the wonder of it all—the Magician's Performance! This can be given by you (with a little know-how and practice as discussed later in the instructions) or by a hired magician (a high school student can be very economical and entertaining). Fifteen magical minutes will have the children bouncing out of their seats and bubbling over with questions . . . "How did he do that?" . . . Giving away no secrets, the magician wishes the children to the birthday table. Here, serve a cake that mimics the invitation—with a bunny's head popping out of a hat—to provide the proper feast and the means for a disappearing act!

While you slice the cake, the children can practice some magical incantations in preparation for the grand finale—the Children's Magic Show. For this, a giant refrigerator box is wrapped with black crepe paper and decorated with silver-foil stars and colorful tissue paper. Unbeknownst to the children, inside the box is an adult, loaded down with goodies! Each child takes a turn at the box, waving a Magic Wand and chanting a magical saying. The results are magical in every way—the children are showered with goodies, and laughter and excitement abound.

 **Out of a Magical Hat**

Out of a magical hat pops a bunny to bring the news of a marvelous, mysterious magic party. While waiting for the party day to arrive, the children can practice with their pop-up bunny invitations and really get into the magical spirit.

Materials: Black and white poster board (1 piece for every 12 invitations); colored markers or crayons; small wiggle eyes; glue; black and silver Con-Tact paper (optional); envelopes; ruler.

To make the pattern: Draw the outline of the hat on paper, as shown in Figure A; cut out. Trace the bunny shown in Figure B; using a ruler, draw

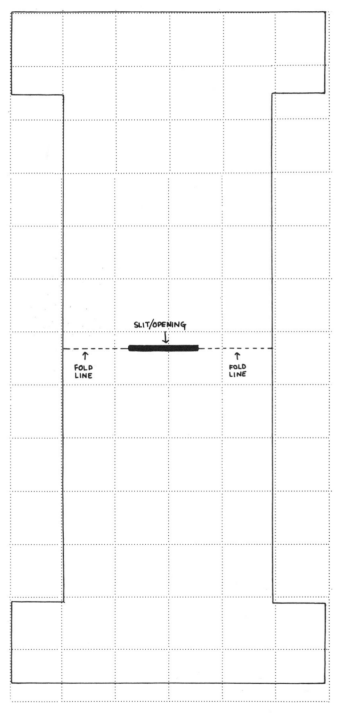

Figure A (1 sq. = 1 in.)

Figure B

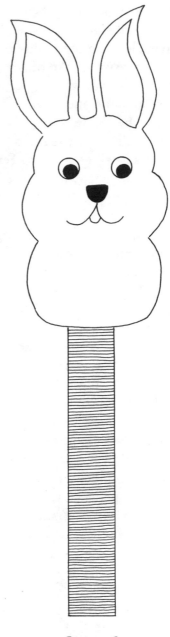

Figure C

a 1 x 5½-inch rectangle at the bottom edge of the bunny to form a hand stick, as shown in Figure C; cut out. Transfer the cutout patterns onto cardboard, drawing along the outlines; cut out. Use these cardboard pieces as the templates for making the invitations.

For each invitation: Trace the hat template on black poster board and the bunny template on white poster board; cut out. To complete the hat,

fold it in half along the fold line; then in the middle of the fold, cut a 1½-inch opening as shown (see Figure A). Open up the hat, then squeeze a thin line of glue along the inside edges of the hat, making sure not to glue the opening in the brim of the hat. Fold the hat along the fold line, glue side in, and secure both sides of the hat together. Cut out and affix a silver Con-Tact paper star on the center of the hat, if desired. To complete the bunny, color the nose, mouth, whiskers, and hand stick with markers or crayons; glue on the wiggle eyes. If desired, you can cover the hand stick with a piece of black Con-Tact paper. Write the party information on the back of the bunny's head. Slide the bunny into the hat, pushing the hand stick through the opening in the fold (see Figure D).

Text: Abracadabra! Please appear at (child's name)'s magical birthday celebration! Time, Date, Place, R.S.V.P.

Marvelous, Mysterious Top Hat

The marvelous, mysterious top hat will certainly add to the magical powers (not to mention the pride) of the wearer. It's as easy to make as peanut butter sandwiches and fits heads of all sizes.

Materials: Black poster board (1 piece for every 2 hats); silver Con-Tact paper; round-cord elastic; tape; black fabric tape (optional); hole puncher.

To make the pattern: Draw the outline of the hat and star as shown in Figure E (page 124). Trace the brim piece (see Figure F, page 125) shown in the pattern section at the back of the book on paper; cut out. Transfer the cutout patterns onto cardboard; cut out. Use these cardboard pieces as the templates for making the hats.

For each hat: Trace the hat and brim templates on black poster board and the star template on silver Con-Tact paper; cut out the pieces. To fit the brim to the hat base, bend the notched (inner) edge up on a 90-degree angle to the brim and place this edge along the inside, lower edge of the hat, curving the hat to fit. Tape (see back view, Figure G, page 125). To complete, affix the star to the front of the hat. If desired, cover the notches and tape along the inner brim edge with a long piece of fabric tape. Punch a hole at the ends of the straight band and tie together with a 6-inch piece of round-cord elastic (see back view, Figure G). Alakazam! You've got a magician's hat (see front view, Figure G).

Figure D

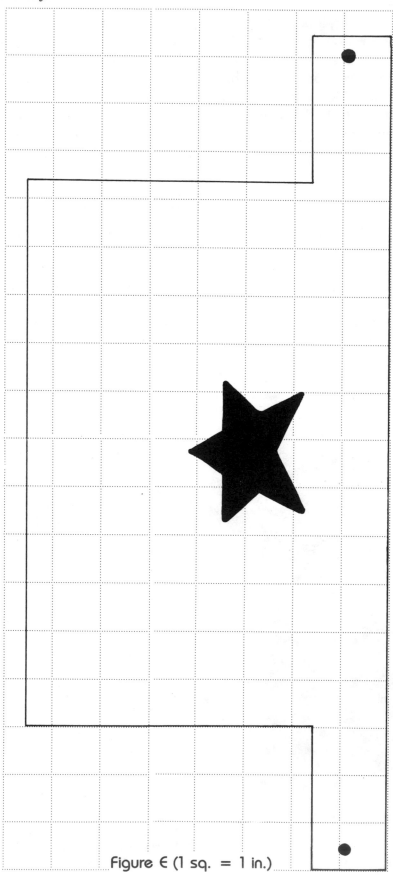

Figure E (1 sq. = 1 in.)

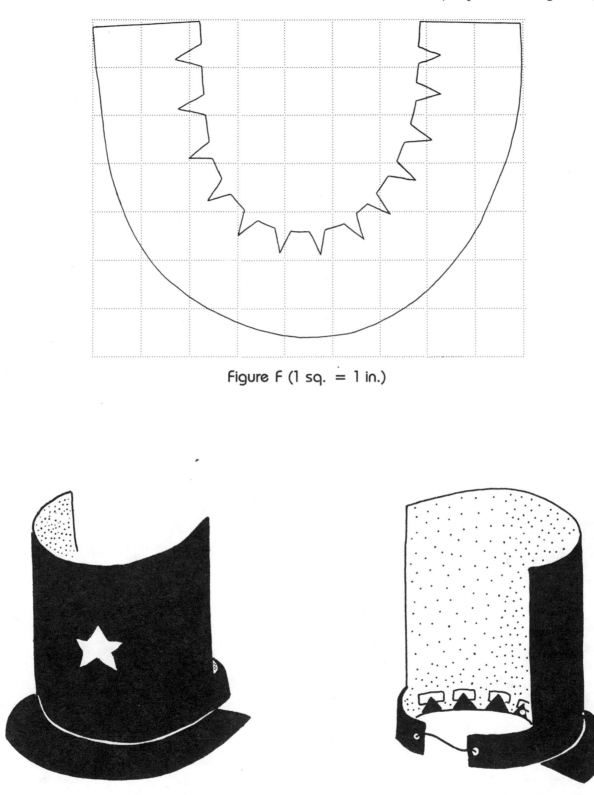

Figure F (1 sq. = 1 in.)

HAT BACK

Figure G

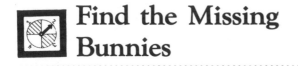 Find the Missing Bunnies

Every magician needs props to perform his magic, and it's just this need that serves as a great excuse for a hunt.

Before the party, hide paper cutout bunnies that have been traced from Figure B (see the invitation instructions) and cut out, or hide pennies or peanuts. At party time, send the children off in all directions, with bags in hand, in search of the missing "props." Have extra bunnies (pennies, peanuts) to hide during the search, so that no one comes back empty-handed. Award each child with a magician's cape and top hat for helping to allow the show to go on.

You can create a treasure hunt, using the traced and cut bunnies as above; write a clue or glue a picture clue on the back of the bunny, leading the children from one bunny to the next. At the end, reward their efforts by handing out the capes and hats.

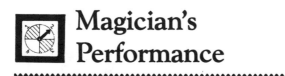 Magician's Performance

It takes a little bit of time and practice, but you can become proficient enough in magic to fool and delight the young ones! One of the keys to success—besides learning the tricks—is to tell a good story. This helps to take some of the attention away from the magical movements and sets the mood, too!

You can get ideas for tricks from books (check your local library), use the ones discussed in this chapter, and purchase others. Most toy stores carry a variety of magical supplies. Practice alone in front of a mirror and in front of someone who won't be a guest at the party. Most of all, have fun and ham it up! Remember, you'll be performing for a young, fascinated audience, not a bunch of professional critics. Here are a few tricks you might want to try.

Balloon-pop trick: Insert a red balloon inside a blue balloon. Inflate them both, the inner (red) balloon less than the blue. Conceal a pin in your hand and, with some fancy hand motions and an alakazoo or two, touch the pin to the blue balloon, being careful not to touch the red one. Bang! The blue balloon explodes, leaving the red one intact (see Figure H). You've changed a blue balloon into a red one. Now that's magic!

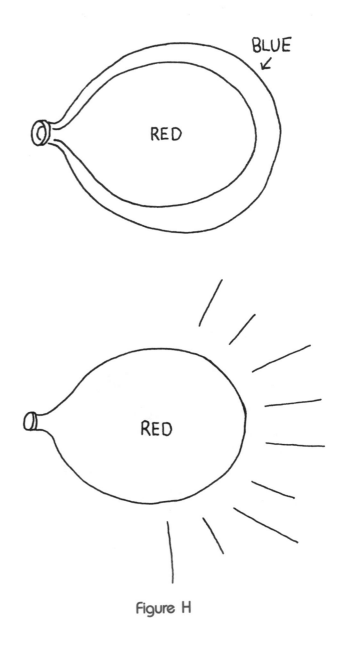

Figure H

Twirling egg: Place a bowl of uncooked eggs on the table and ask a few children to try and spin an egg. No one will succeed. Then you try but use an egg that has been hard-boiled (don't let anyone know). To everyone's amazement, your egg will spin (see Figure I).

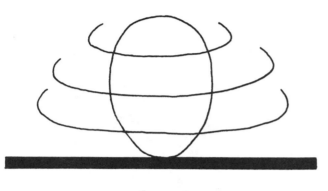

Figure I

Vanishing pencil: Hold a pencil upright in your hand (see Figure J). Place the handkerchief over the pencil so it covers your hand. While adjusting the handkerchief, substitute your forefin- ger for the pencil, letting the pencil slide into your sleeve. Your forefinger will now be propping up the handkerchief instead of the pencil (see Figure K). Perform a few magical incantations and moves and wave the handkerchief away. The pencil has vanished!

At performance time: Have everything set up and ready to use on a surface that children can easily see. Keep in mind these important tips while performing (they will add to the success of your show): (1) give the children a feeling of won- der—share in their amazement; (2) keep the secret of the illusion—most of the fun is in the believ- ing; and (3) don't tell the children in advance what you're going to do. It adds to the surprise and deception. Gather the children together around the "stage" area and, dressed in your magi- cal garb (cape and hat or perhaps a tuxedo if you own one), tell the audience your name and get on with the show!

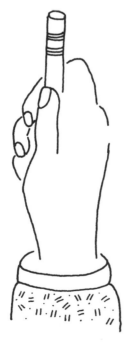

Figure J

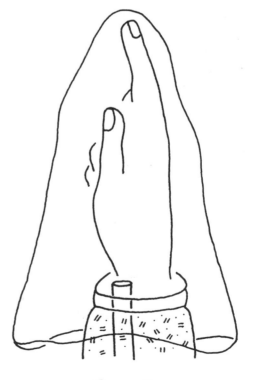

Figure K

Children's Magic Show

Since the children will have their own magician's outfits, why not let them get into the act? Try out this fun activity, and you'll have them all believing they have a little magic inside themselves! To do it, you create a giant magic box out of which pop crazy and wonderful things when each child waves a wand and chants a hocus-pocus or two. It's extremely simple to make, and the rewards are almost too good to be true!

Materials: Refrigerator box (usually available at appliance stores); black crepe paper (about 5 packages); aluminum foil; tape; colorful tissue paper; soft things for throwing—streamers, confetti, marshmallows, balloons, ribbons, tissue-paper balls, Gummi Bears, pom-poms, cotton balls, bubbles, etc.

To transform the refrigerator box into a magical box: First cut out a door on one side, large enough for an adult to slip into the box; remove the box top. Cover the box with crepe paper, wrapping it around the box and taping it in back near the door. Add a strip or two of foil, if desired, and tape a large foil star in the center front of the box. To complete the outside decoration, gather up some sheets of tissue paper and tuck them inside the bottom end flap, forming a "ruffle" along the bottom edge of the box (see front view, Figure L). Inside the box, tape paper bags for holding some of the goodies that will fly out of the top of the box during the performance. When choosing the goodies, such as those listed in the materials, just be sure that they are soft enough so they won't hurt anyone who gets hit as the object flies through the air (plastic figures, balls, etc., are not good choices).

At party time: An adult or other helper slips inside the box inconspicuously, right before the magical event. Armed with and surrounded by

FRONT VIEW

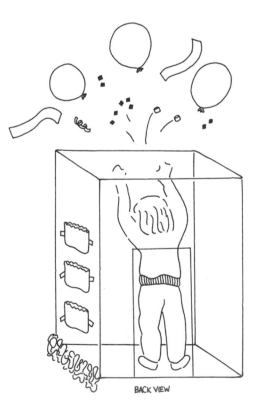

BACK VIEW

Figure L

the goodies, the helper throws out the confetti, balloons, etc. (one type of thing at a time) as each child performs a magical chant and wand-waving motions (see back view, Figure L). All the children can partake of the goodies, if they can stop giggling long enough to collect them!

Make a Magical Wand

Let each child decorate a special magic wand—a poster-board star bedecked with glitter, ribbons, and other fancy stuff.

Materials: Red and yellow poster board (or any 2 contrasting colors); double-stick tape; glue; cotton swabs; fuzzy pipe cleaners; glitter, paper squiggles, feathers, beads, felt scraps, sequins, and other gobbledygook; hole puncher.

To make the pattern: Trace the wand outline shown in the pattern section at the back of the book. See Figure M; cut out. Transfer the cutout pattern onto cardboard; cut out. Use this cardboard piece as the template for making the magic wands.

To make each wand: Trace the template on yellow and red poster board; cut out. Using double-stick tape or glue, stick the 2 wand pieces together, lining up the edges (don't worry if they don't line up perfectly, a little bit of contrasting color peeking through looks great). Punch a hole in both lower star points and lace a halved piece of pipe cleaner through. Thread some beads, felt pieces, or other fancy things through the pipe cleaner and twist closed to form a loop (see Figure M).

Assemble the decorations—glitter, feathers, paper squiggles, etc.—and put them in a bowl or cup for each child.

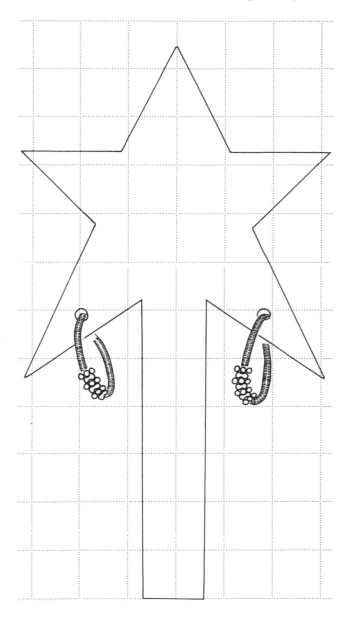

Figure M (1 sq. = 1 in.)

At party time: Give each child a wand, a portion of decorative goodies, and a small square of cardboard with a blob of glue and a glue stick (craft stick or cotton swab without cotton) to spread the glue with. Let them "go to town," making their wands as decorative as they want. The results will be quite magical!

Magician's Cape

Who can perform magic without a cape—it adds a bit of flair and professionalism to the wearer! This one can be made in a flash, so don't even consider getting along without it!

Materials: Black felt (½ yard of 72-inch felt for 2 capes); thread; ¾-inch-wide ribbon (about 1½ yards per cape); safety pin; square of yellow felt (optional).

For each cape: Cut out an 18 x 36-inch rectangle of black felt. Turn under 2¾ inches along one edge; stitch close to the edge and then again, 1¾ inches away (towards the fold) to form a casing (see Figure N). Attach a safety pin to one edge of the ribbon and pull the ribbon through the casing (see Figure N). Gather up the cape, leaving about 14 inches of ribbon exposed on each side; tack in place with a few stitches. To add a bit more pizzazz, cut a star out of yellow felt and glue it on the center back of the cape. Put it on the wearer and tie a big bow! Terrific!

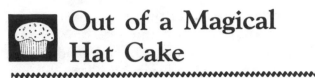

Out of a Magical Hat Cake

Out of a magical hat comes an edible bunny, too. This easy magic trick starts with a 9 x 13-inch cake made from a mix!

Materials: One 9 x 13-inch cake (see Cake Tips in "How to Use This Book"); 1 can or 1 recipe white frosting; 1 can or ½ recipe chocolate frosting; red food coloring to make pink frosting; candies for the bunny's features—licorice laces for the whiskers and mouth, jelly circles for the eyebrows and eyes, spice drops for the tongue and nose (or candies of your choice).

To finish the cake: Following the pattern in Figure O, draw a full-size pattern for each of the pieces and cut out. Lay the pattern pieces directly on the cake and cut along the edges with a sharp, large knife, keeping it as vertical as possible when cutting. Lay the hat piece on a large platter or cardboard piece covered with foil; assemble the cake—as shown in Figure P—affixing the bunny

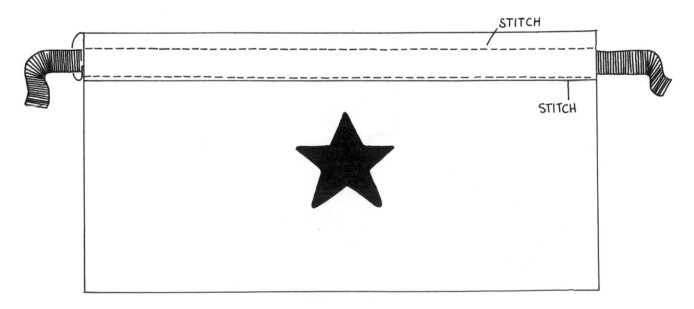

Figure N

head to the center of the hat brim, the ears to the bunny, and the brim pieces to the hat. Use some of the frosting to "glue" the pieces together. Frost the bunny head and ears white. Tint the remaining white frosting pink for the inner ears and the star; use the chocolate frosting for the hat. Frost as shown in Figure P (see page 132). To complete, add the candy pieces for the facial features and poof—your cake is ready to enchant!

While cutting the cake, have the children take turns making up magical chants. The wait for the dessert won't seem so long!

Suggestions

As mentioned, there are numerous commercially available tricks and books, wands, and other magical-looking things, such as disappearing ink and code pens, whoopie cushions, buzzers, camera squirt guns, can of worms, trick candy, etc., which can be found in novelty, toy, and magic shops. Keep these in mind when buying treats, prizes, or favors and when looking for substitutions for party elements described in this chapter.

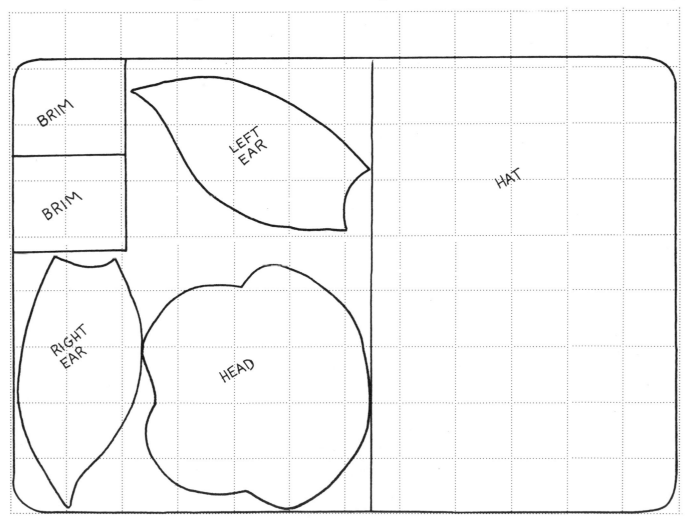

Figure O (1 sq. = 1 in.)

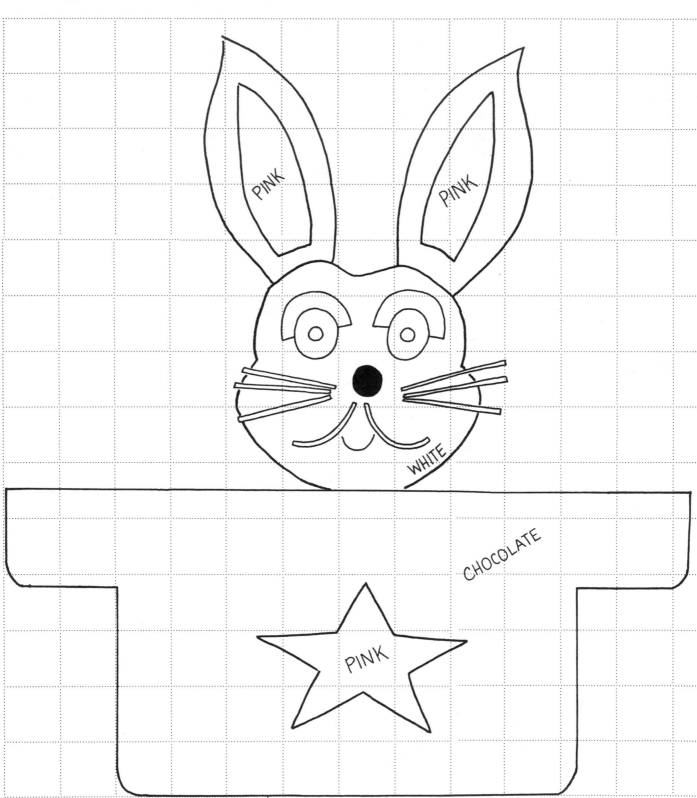

Figure P (1 sq. = 1 in.)

LARGE PATTERNS

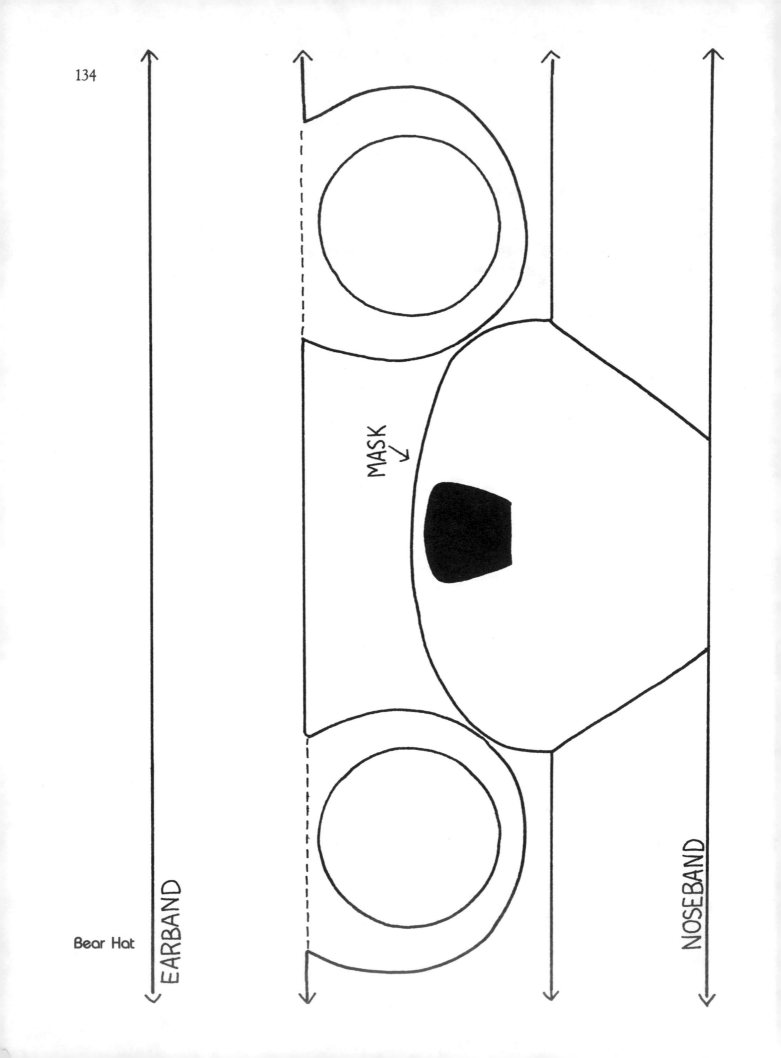

134

Bear Hat

EARBAND

MASK

NOSEBAND

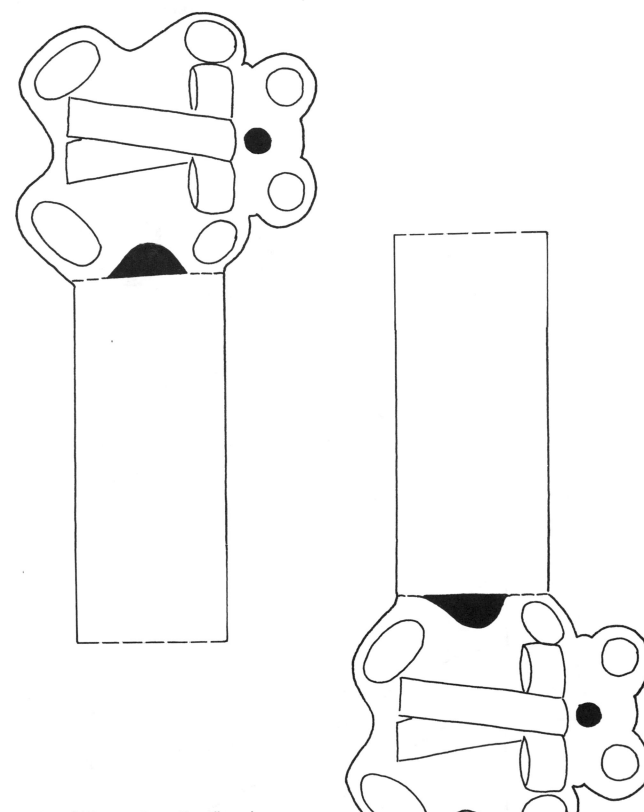

Wear-a-Bear Headband
(Attach sections at center
to make one-piece pattern)

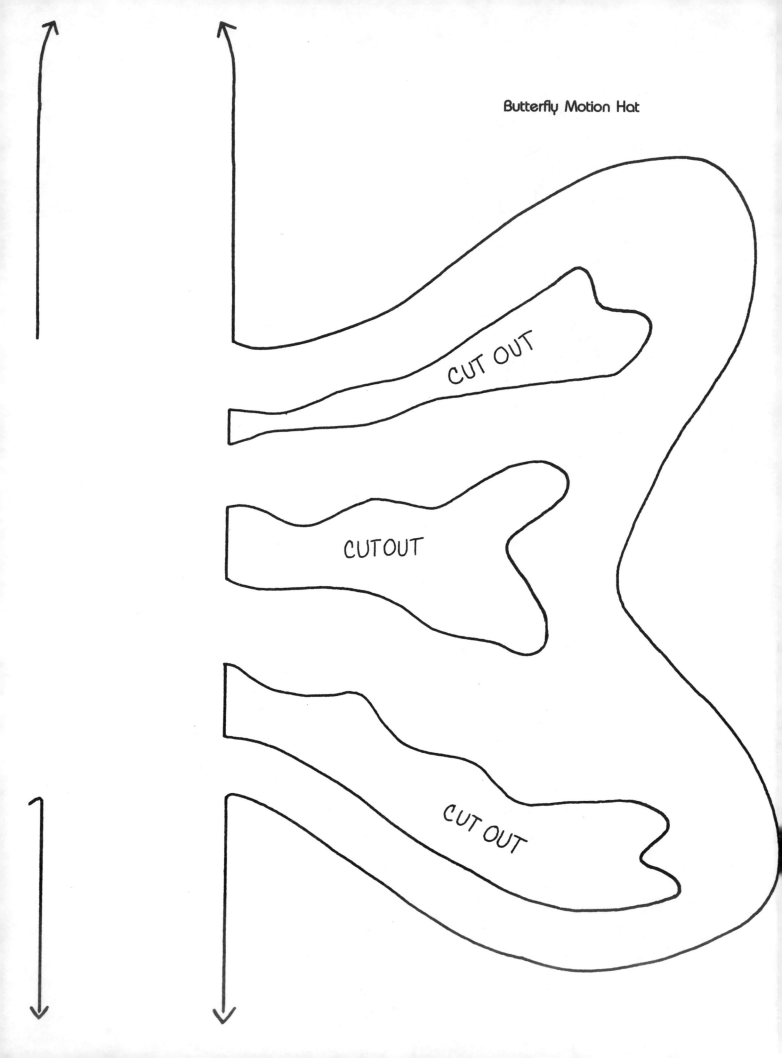

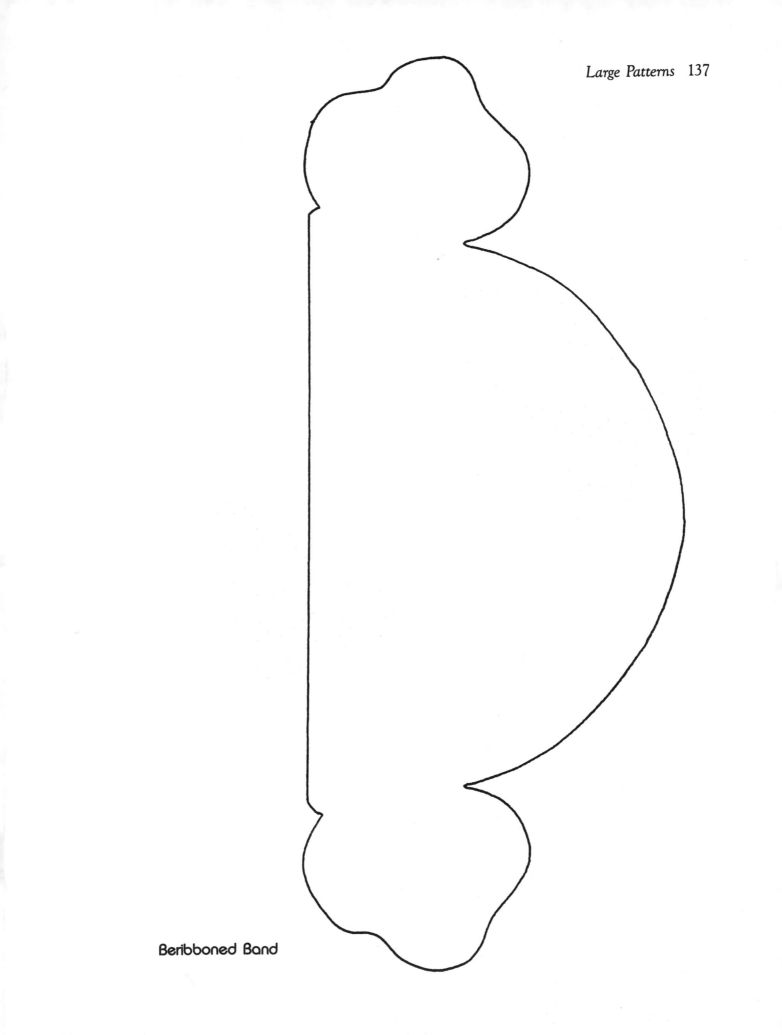

Beribboned Band

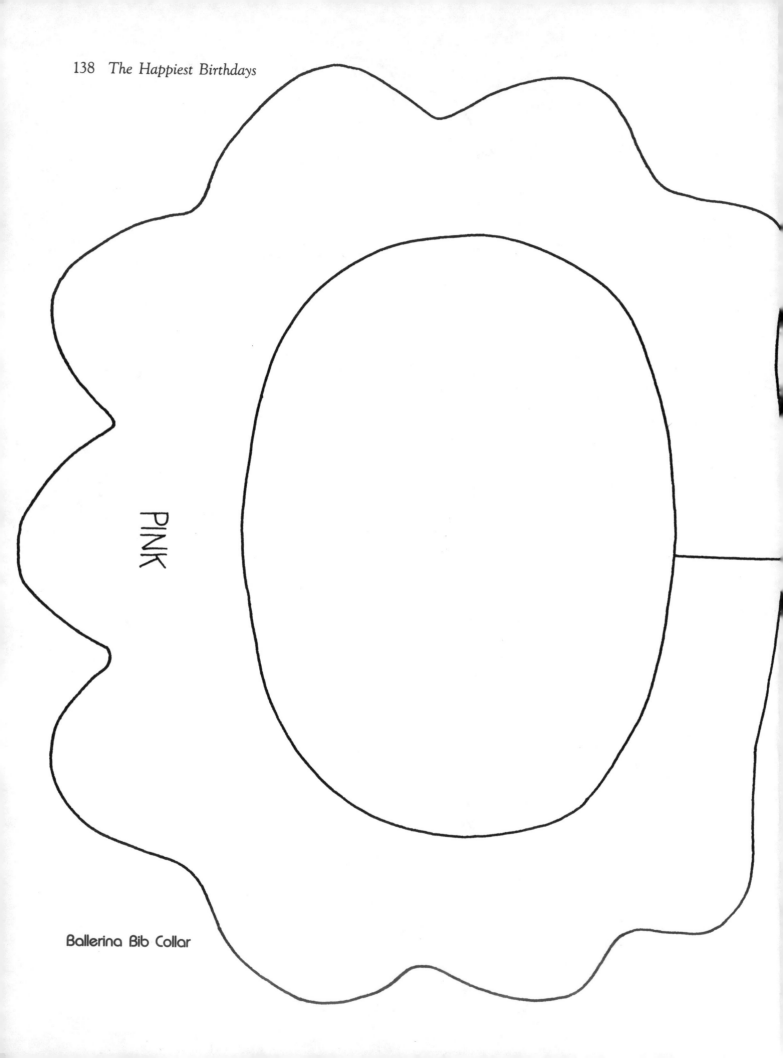

PINK

Ballerina Bib Collar

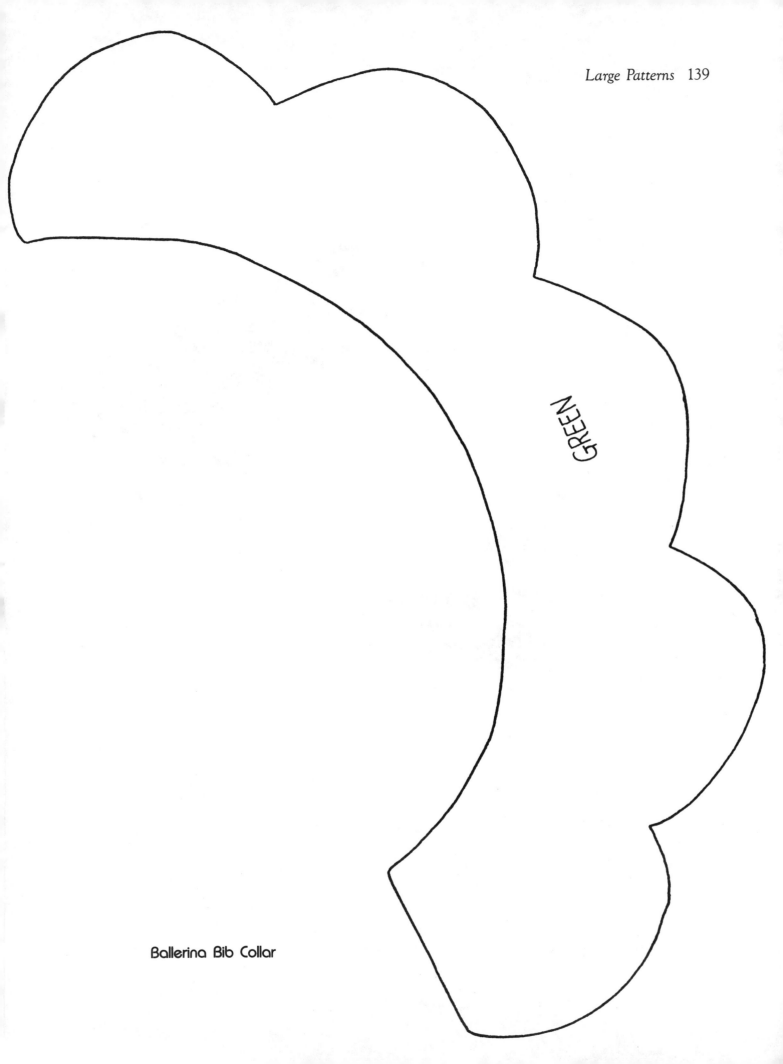

GREEN

Ballerina Bib Collar

Dino Head

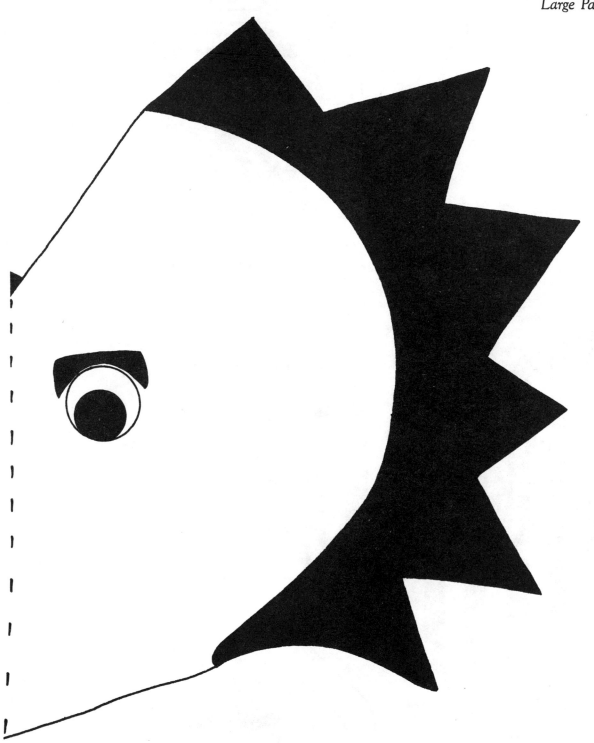

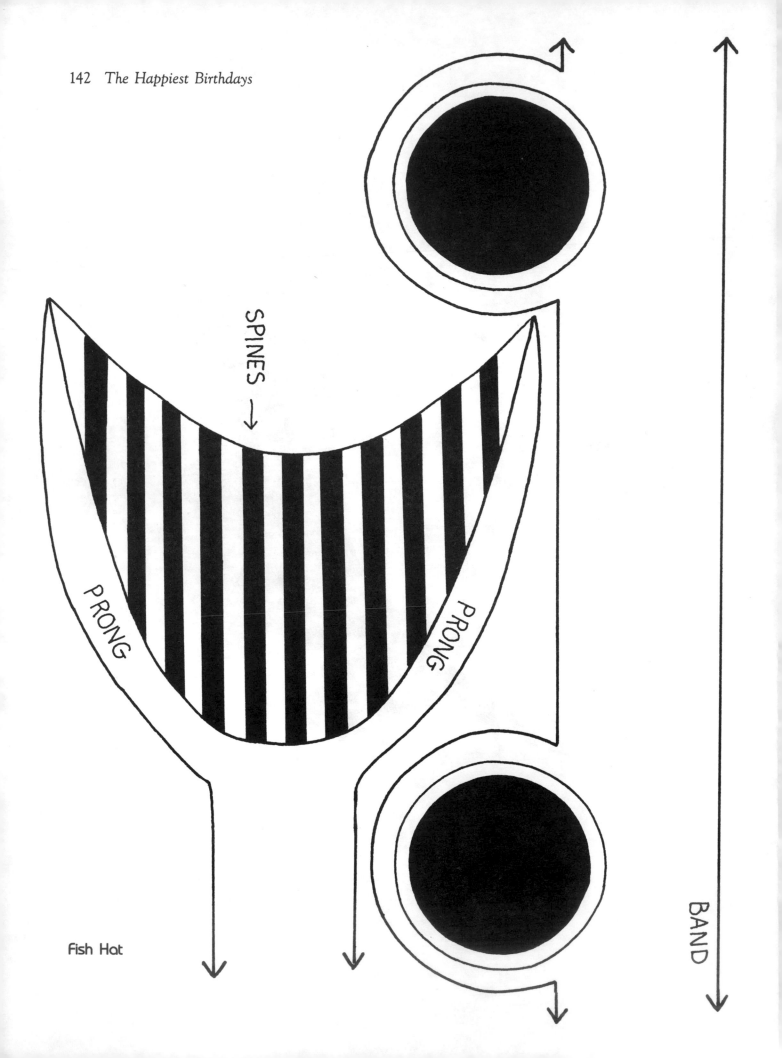

SPINES →

PRONG

PRONG

BAND

Fish Hat

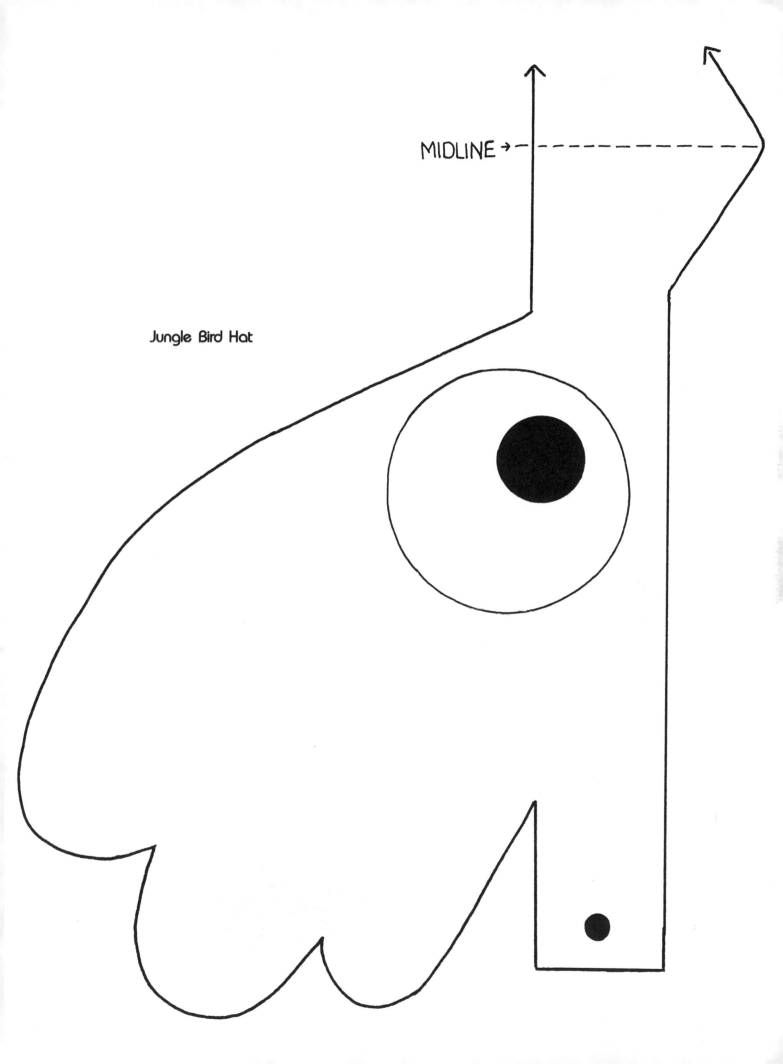

MIDLINE →

Jungle Bird Hat

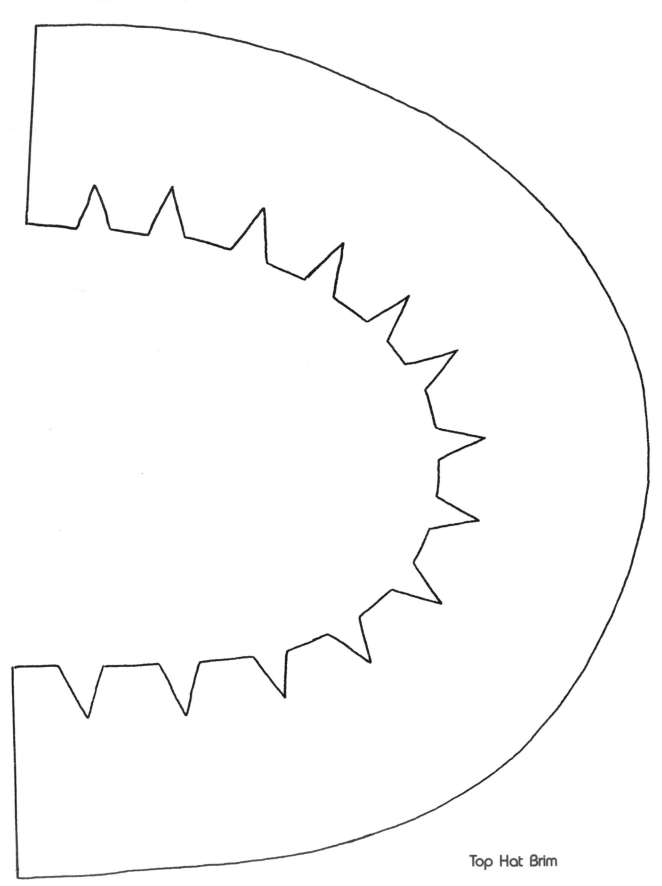

Top Hat Brim

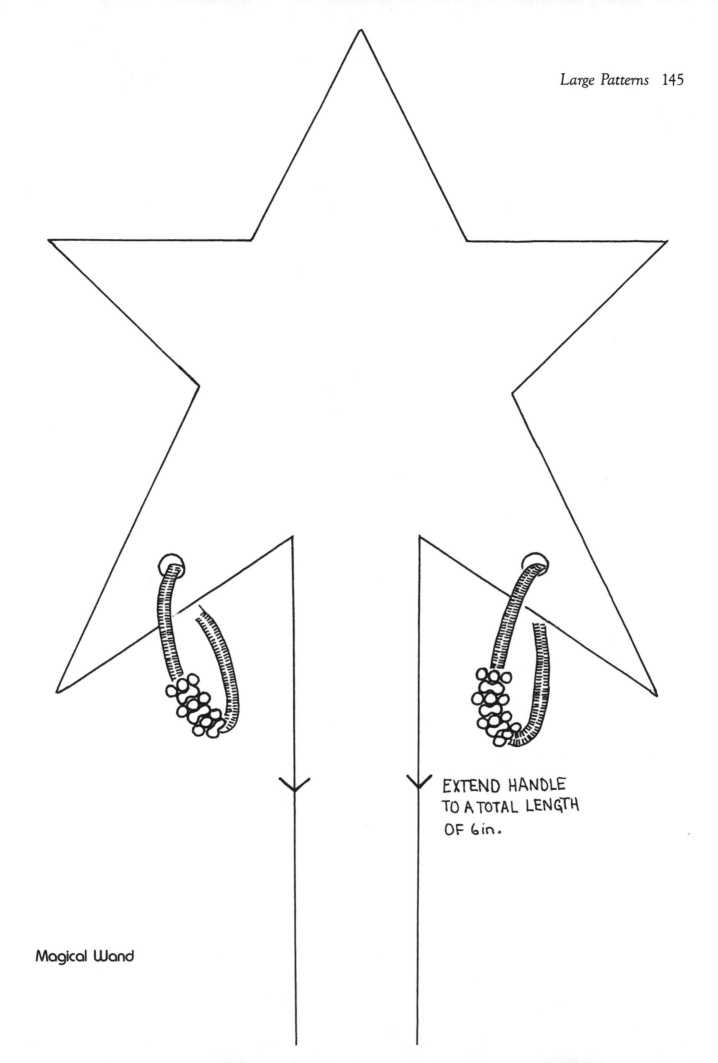

EXTEND HANDLE
TO A TOTAL LENGTH
OF 6 in.

Magical Wand